HIGH INTEREST READING

BIOGRAPHIES

by Delana Heidrich

Illustrated by
Don O'Connor

Cover by
Don O'Connor

Cover design by
Peggy Jackson

Publisher
Instructional Fair • TS Denison
Grand Rapids, MI 49544

ISBN: 0-7424-0132-4
High Interest Reading: Biographies

a Division of Instructional Fair Group, Inc.
3195 Wilson Dr. NW
Grand Rapids, Michigan 49544

Introduction

Middle school students love a juicy story. A true tale of triumph over poverty, misfortune, bad choices, or failures makes a juicy story. Learning that Abraham Lincoln was a lousy postal clerk before becoming one of our most beloved presidents feels more like listening to gossip than reading history. Uncovering the rags-to-riches life of Hans Christian Andersen resembles reading a fairy tale more than plodding through a biography.

High Interest Reading: Biographies is full of good, juicy stories about the bumps along life's road as encountered by men and women. Students will recognize these individuals by their eventual successes in literature, politics, business, sports, or the arts. Fascinated readers will discover that Babe Ruth was considered incorrigible by his own parents. They will learn that the author of the fastest computer program in the world withstood civil war and refugee camp living in Nigeria before ever being introduced to a computer. Additionally, they will investigate the tragic life of Thomas Paine and the slow, failure-filled start in the life of Mr. Milton Hershey, creator of the chocolate kiss.

Each alluring student reading is preceded by an informative teacher page and followed by two or three subject-related student activities. All teacher pages include background reading material, explanations of student activities, and a list of extension ideas. All student pages include complete instructions and self-contained activities that require few or no outside reference materials.

Use the readings and activities as extra credit, homework, or supplemental assignments in conjunction with history or language arts studies.

Table of Contents

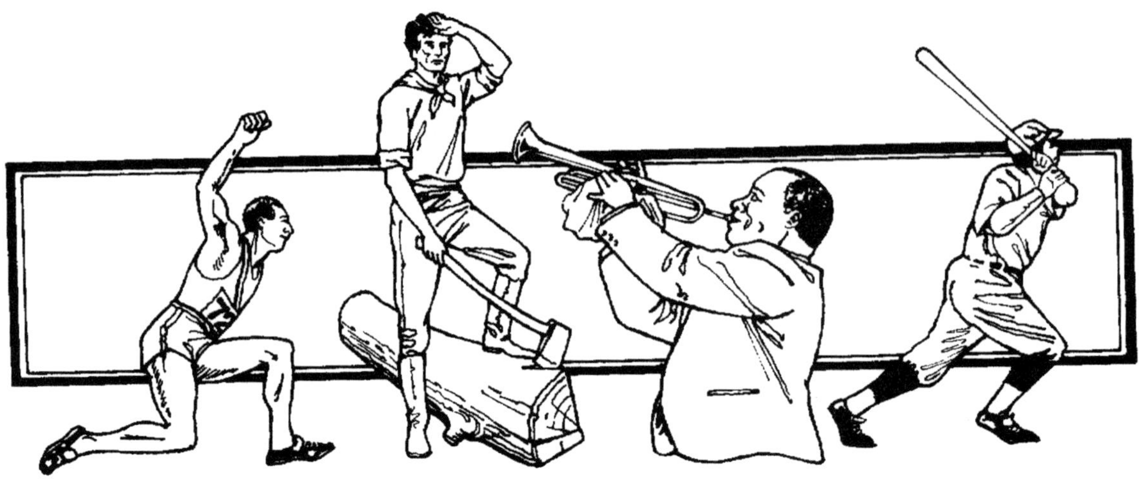

Tilting at Windmills

Background

Miguel de Cervantes Saavedra lived in exciting times in the history of Spain. Just 50 years prior to his birth, Spain had fought its way into the position of a major European power under the rule of King Ferdinand. By the time Miguel had celebrated his third birthday in 1550, his motherland had discovered, explored, and conquered most of the South American continent in addition to Central America, Florida, Cuba, and the Philippine Islands. During Cervantes' adulthood his country conducted an anti-French campaign, initiated a series of battles against Italy that established Spain's dominance in that country, led the efforts of an alliance called the Holy League, fighting off Turkish threats to the politically powerful Christian church, and established a magnificent fleet of 130 battleships to be used in an attempt to overtake England.

Cervantes got caught up in the times. He fought bravely aboard a tossing ship in the Battle of Lepanto. He requisitioned wheat and olive oil from Spanish farmers in patriotic support of his country's Armada. He spent five years in Algiers as one of many prisoners of Barbary pirates who overtook a boat on which he was sailing.

Adventurous, yes, but the life of Miguel de Cervantes was not successful until the man reached his fiftieth year. Even then, when Cervantes wrote what is considered the world's first true novel, Spain's best literary work, and a masterpiece in world literature, he received little financial compensation for his achievement. When French diplomats visiting Madrid in the early 1600s asked where they might find the author of the classic Don Quixote series, they were directed to the undistinguished home of a long-forgotten, poverty-stricken old man.

In this lesson students read about the fascinating life and accomplishments of author Miguel de Cervantes Saavedra and then complete activities based on the reading.

Teaching Activities

Modern Adventures: Students imagine the adventures Don Quixote might experience in today's world.
Defining Descriptions: Students practice identifying a number of setting descriptions.

Extensions

1. Assign students the reading and summarizing of sections of one of the *Don Quixote* stories.
2. Assign the writing of tall-tale, adventure stories.
3. Assign the writing of a short story that champions moral actions through a satirical or humorous storyline.
4. Assign the writing of stories featuring knights and maidens as main characters.
5. Cervantes put the life he lived to work for him in his writing. Require students to write poems that reflect experiences from their own lives.
6. Assign the creation of time lines that reflect the real-life adventures of Miguel de Cervantes Saavedra.
7. Conduct a study of Spanish history or of Spain's current politics, geography, and population.
8. Research the Holy League and the strange mix between politics and religion in sixteenth-century Spain. Continue learning about religion and politics by studying the region's history from the present back to the days of the Crusades.

Student Reading

Tilting at Windmills

Miguel de Cervantes Saavedra did not live the quiet life of a feverish writer confined to the book-lined study of a world-class author. In fact, the creator of Spain's most celebrated literary character did not even sit still long enough to dream up his legendary Don Quixote until he was beyond his fiftieth year of life. Prior to that time, Cervantes was more of an outdoorsman.

Born near Madrid, Spain, in 1547, Miguel de Cervantes was welcomed into a poverty-stricken family. Although few specifics are known about his early life, it has been determined that Cervantes was the son of a traveling surgeon who treated more poor patients than paying ones. Even Papa Cervantes' periodic sacrifices of personal belongings to area pawnshops could not always keep the man out of debtor's prison. Miguel Cervantes spent more time traveling from town to town with his parents and six siblings while scrounging for food and clothing than he did attending school as a boy.

Perhaps then, it was the monetary security of military life which appealed to Cervantes when he grew into a young man. As he trained with the Italian navy before the outset of the Battle of Lepanto, which pitted the Holy League against her Turkish aggressor, he found himself eating three meals a day while dressed in a fine military uniform. It must have felt like heaven until he set foot on his company's battleship staged for war. Before the first cannon fired, Cervantes came down with malarial fever. As the Lepanto battle began, he lay below deck in agony. Still he rose with valor to join his fellow soldiers in sinking Turkish ships, capturing over 100 galleys, and freeing thousands of Christian slaves. In the end 8,000 Christians lay dead alongside 25,000 Turks. Cervantes was only slightly more fortunate than the conflict's victims. Two bullets struck the sick soldier in the chest, while a third penetrated his left arm and rendered that limb (including hand and fingers) useless for the rest of his life. Other hardships were close behind.

While returning to Spain, the ship Cervantes occupied was overtaken by Barbary pirates who sailed the vessel to Algiers and sold its sailors into slavery. Unfortunately, Cervantes carried with him a letter of recommendation written by a superior in the Battle of Lepanto. Because of this letter, his new owner thought he must be an important man, and he requested a high ransom from Cervantes' family. It took them and a group of Trinitarian friars five years to raise enough money to answer the request.

Cervantes was disappointed that he was not offered a military post in thanks for his service in the Holy League. When he finally reached Spanish soil again, he tried his hand at writing. Although his single pastoral story and few plays earned him a little money, they did not provide him the kind of cash he needed to repay the friars who rescued him from bondage.

So from about 1585 until 1604, he turned to working for the crown. For awhile he held the dangerous post of a requisitioner of wheat and olive oil to supply the Spanish Armada. Farmers were none too happy to relinquish their goods to the military, and Cervantes was mocked, threatened, and excommunicated from his church while carrying out the duties of that job. Next he attempted to obtain permission to immigrate to the New World but was turned down. So he accepted a post as tax collector, but in that position, Cervantes demonstrated a lack of knowledge about economics. Sloppy bookkeeping landed him in prison on two different occasions.

Fortunately, during his last stay behind bars, Cervantes returned to writing. This time he did not attempt romanticized stories of shepherds and shepherdesses as he did in his pastoral. He did not pen plays that could be rejected by local theaters. He instead wrote what he knew—travel, captivity, war, and high adventure on land and at sea.

In a humorous parody of stories of chivalry, Miguel Cervantes also wrote of the relationship and the value of realism and idealism. *El ingenioso hidalgo Don Quixote de la Mancha* became an instant success. Readers all over the continent became familiar with the antics of Don Quixote. Within two weeks of the publication of Cervantes' remarkable tale of a man who reads so many stories about knights that he imagines himself to be one, three unauthorized editions appeared on the market and claimed much of the wealth Cervantes should have received with his success. In fact, although the next two Don Quixote stories were also great successes with the public, as were the other works he wrote from 1605 until his death in 1616, Miguel de Cervantes died a rather poor man.

In his lifetime, Cervantes gained some fame, but did not live long enough to learn of the lasting significance of his writings. The original Don Quixote story is considered the world's first novel. Instead of being written with cardboard characters who made predictable decisions for the sole purpose of making a point, the book was written with fully developed characters who interacted with the imaginary world of the story as real people might. Authors to follow Cervantes learned much from his style.

Today *El ingenioso hidalgo Don Quixote de la Mancha* is considered one of the masterpieces of world literature along with the works of Homer and Shakespeare. It has been translated into countless languages and analyzed by generations of scholars. Dreamers and idealists continue to be accused of "tilting at windmills" as Don Quixote did when he imagined them to be giants. Even people who no longer remember his adventures know the name of Don Quixote. A man who claimed little personal success in the course of his lifetime created a character who continues to flourish today.

Name ______________________________

Modern Adventures

The character Don Quixote is an old man who reads so many tales of chivalry that he convinces himself he is a knight with the mission to right the world's wrongs. His less educated (but more sane) neighbor Sancho Panza accompanies Don Quixote on adventures throughout Spain in the Middle Ages. Along the way, Don Quixote is often mistaking peasants for noblemen or everyday objects for enemies. Sancho Panza calmly corrects his master's mistakes but is always ignored. For example, in one scene, Don Quixote is convinced that a field of windmills is a field of many-armed giants. Sancho Panza is unable to dissuade Don Quixote of his belief, so Quixote attacks a windmill with his lance and ends up being thrown to the ground along with his horse. Following the attack of the windmill, Don Quixote concludes that some imagined enemy must have turned the giants into windmills at the last moment because he did not want to be upstaged by Don Quixote's ability to ward off an entire field full of giants.

What kind of trouble might Don Quixote get into in today's world were he imagining modern people and things to be things they were not? Outline his possible adventures when meeting the people or items listed below. The first one has been completed for you as an example.

Real Person or Item Encountered	Person or Item Don Quixote Imagines It to Be	Results of Mistaken Identity
an airplane	a huge, high-flying attack bird	Quixote shoots an arrow at the "bird" which flies away in what Quixote takes to be fright.
an automobile	______________	______________
a policeman in uniform	______________	______________
an electric fan	______________	______________
a skyscraper	______________	______________
a doctor carrying medical instruments	______________	______________

Name ______________________

Defining Descriptions

In addition to offering readers humor and philosophical insights, the *Don Quixote* tales provide a rich description of fourteenth-century Spain. How much attention do you pay to the descriptions in a story? Match the following descriptive paragraphs with the settings they describe.

Settings

CLASSROOM CAMPGROUND MOVIE THEATER CITY LIBRARY

______________ 1. The lake was one solid block of ice this time of year. The trees surrounding it were bare except for the crystallized snowflakes that glistened on their branches. The outdoor temperature seldom topped 25 degrees, but the fishermen and hunters did not seem to mind. They bundled up in their full-length snowsuits by day and crowded around their cabins' fireplaces by night.

______________ 2. Rush hour always made Carolyn nervous. Horns honked, brakes screeched, and drivers yelled out their windows at fellow drivers who cut in from side streets or at throngs of pedestrians who continued to cross at intersections even after the light changed. Carolyn anxiously anticipated leaving the skyscrapers and shopping malls and noise and hustle and bustle behind for the weekend. How relieved she would be if only the single-file parking lot she found herself in would inch forward enough for her to hit the freeway.

______________ 3. The click, click, clicking of women's high heels echoed on the hardwood floor of the enormous old building. Shelves and shelves of musty old books could not absorb their insistent tapping. Then there were the hushed squeals of glee coming from the children enjoying story time in the corner. On a nearby bench, an old woman crumpled her newspaper with each page turn while her companion cleared his throat or blew his nose every 30 seconds. Why did they have to make a quiet rule in places like this? Maybe a little talk would cover up the shoe clicking and nose blowing and allow Meagan to get a little studying done.

______________ 4. The annoying ringing of the tardy bell signaled Tommy to take his seat. He best take out his notebook and pencil. The overhead projector in the front of the room assured him that Mr. Pencilton would be lecturing again today.

______________ 5. The lights dim slowly as the screen lights up in a sudden flash of multiple colors. The almost life-size image and surround sound of a loud-whistling train make Grandma sit up in her plush red chair with the cup holder on the armrest. Before the first preview is even over, she is reaching for popcorn to munch on slowly as her eyes pop out in fear. Grandma really needs to get out more!

Rags to Riches: A Fairy-Tale Life

Background

Citizens of late eighteenth- and early nineteenth-century Europe had grown accustomed to astonishing transformations. They had witnessed cottage industries, which produced a few one-of-a-kind garments by hand, change to weaving and spinning mill factories that mass-produced clothes faster than the locals could buy them. They had lived through expansions in world trade that changed the very face of industry, economy, and international politics. Citizens of late eighteenth- and early nineteenth-century Europe watched the fall of absolute monarchies, the death of feudalism, the rise of democracy, and the power of conquest as Napoleon marched across the continent.

Nearly incomprehensible changes were initiated with James Watt's improvements on the steam engine in 1765. These changes continued throughout the French Revolution of 1789 and must have made citizens of the time period feel they were characters in a live fairy tale. Unfair kings and unjust priests lost their heads to the guillotine, while abused and impoverished "Cinderellas" took over the castles and thrones.

So, the great transformation of Hans Christian Andersen, born in the year 1805, may not have completely shocked his contemporaries. Born poor, left fatherless by the age of 11, and turned runaway by the age of 14, Andersen had obtained funds from the king of Denmark by the time he was 28 to wander through Europe telling stories and entertaining fans. By the time of his death at age 70, Andersen had entertained not only common fans on the streets of Europe, but also famous kings, queens, artists, and intellectuals. In a century full of fantastic transformations, an impoverished youth, illiterate for the first 14 years of his life, became the beloved author of 168 fairy tales that entertained the common man and the royalty of his day—and the common man and the royalty of many days to come.

In this lesson students read about the false starts on the way to success in the life of one of the world's most beloved storytellers.

Teaching Activities

Mr. Andersen or Brothers Grimm? Students determine which of the listed stories were written by Hans Christian Andersen and which were written by the Grimm brothers.
From Fact to Fairy Tale: Students read the plots of some Andersen stories that followed loosely the details of his life.
Light Tale, Deep Truths: Students try their own hands at writing important lessons in fairy-tale form.

Extensions

1. Have students read Hans Christian Andersen stories aloud to classmates or younger students at an area school.
2. Compare and contrast stories of fiction including fairy tales, folklore, fantasy, tall tales, fables, historical fiction, and realistic fiction.
3. Assign research and reports on the fairy tales of various nations or on the history of fairy tales in general.
4. Assign students the rewriting of famous tales from memory to be included in a class book of retold tales.
5. Read Hans Christian Andersen novels, autobiographies, poems, or travel stories.

Student Reading

Rags to Riches: A Fairy-Tale Life

Hans Christian Andersen's unmatched ability to write fairy tales might be attributed to his insistence on believing in them. Born in 1805, Hans lived in fairy-tale times. The Industrial Revolution had transformed the world. Machine-produced goods had replaced hand-made products overnight. America had declared its independence. France had embraced democracy. Almost inconceivable life-altering transformations were possible (and happening) on an incredibly large scale.

So perhaps it is not surprising that Hans Christian Andersen did not feel tied to the one-room cottage in which he was born. Even after his father's death when Hans Christian Andersen was 11, he did not feel trapped in his life of poverty. He hoped to be a great and successful man.

Hans was born to an intelligent but unschooled shoemaker and his illiterate wife who worked as a laundress. His father read to him often and encouraged his imagination by building him puppets and toy theater sets. After Hans' father's death, Hans' mother attempted to uphold her husband's dream of educating their son. Young Hans could memorize and recite the stories told by the old ladies that spun thread at the local poorhouse, but he could read and write very little, so he did not fare well in school. Eventually Hans' mother decided her son had best learn a trade instead.

Young Hans failed at one trade after another. He apprenticed unsuccessfully with a weaver, a tobacconist, a tailor, and a shoemaker. Already a four-time failure at the age of 14, he packed his bags and ran away from his jobs to Copenhagen, alone and nearly penniless. He insisted on a life in the performing arts. He wanted to sing, dance, act, and write plays. So he did. Unfortunately, he was too gawky to succeed at dancing or acting. He was successful at singing in a boys' choir only for a few months until his voice changed. And his plays were rejected due to the numerous grammatical and structural errors in the writing of a boy who was nearly illiterate.

At last, after three years of relying on the kindnesses of friends for housing and food, 17-year-old Hans was granted an opportunity to succeed on his own. Jonas Collin, the director of a local theater, saw through the grammatical errors in a Hans Christian Andersen play to the depth of his characters and story plot. He arranged for the boy to attend school. Hans worked for six years alongside children half his age to learn to read and write and understand mathematics. By age 23 he was able to pass the entrance exams to the university in Copenhagen. By age 24 he was publishing stories. Four years later he was accepting funds from the king of Denmark to travel all over Europe sharing his stories with fans.

By the time of his death at the age of 70, Hans Christian Andersen had written 168 fairy tales in addition to varied other works. He had journeyed outside of Denmark 30 times and befriended famous and common folks around the globe. Today the fairy tales of Hans Christian Andersen—the man who lived a fairy-tale life—have been translated into over 100 languages and have been enjoyed by millions.

Name ______________________________

Mr. Andersen or Brothers Grimm?

Hans Christian Andersen wrote many fairy tales whose titles you would recognize, but do you know just which ones? See if you can distinguish between the tales of Mr. Andersen and those German tales that were retold by the famous Grimm brothers. Circle your guess. Then match the tales with their descriptions by placing a letter in the space before each tale.

_____ 1.	*The Little Mermaid*	GRIMM BROTHERS or ANDERSEN
_____ 2.	*The Emperor's New Clothes*	GRIMM BROTHERS or ANDERSEN
_____ 3.	*The Ugly Duckling*	GRIMM BROTHERS or ANDERSEN
_____ 4.	*Rumpelstiltskin*	GRIMM BROTHERS or ANDERSEN
_____ 5.	*The Princess and the Pea*	GRIMM BROTHERS or ANDERSEN
_____ 6.	*The Little Match Girl*	GRIMM BROTHERS or ANDERSEN
_____ 7.	*Hansel and Gretel*	GRIMM BROTHERS or ANDERSEN
_____ 8.	*Rapunzel*	GRIMM BROTHERS or ANDERSEN
_____ 9.	*The Old Woman in the Wood*	GRIMM BROTHERS or ANDERSEN
_____10.	*Thumbelina*	GRIMM BROTHERS or ANDERSEN

Story Descriptions

A. In order to save her life, a young woman is required to enter into a contract with a magic man who can turn straw into gold. Later, to get out of the contract, she is given the task of guessing the magic little man's name.

B. A mermaid falls in love with a man.

C. A young woman frees a prince from an evil witch's spell by retrieving a ring from an old woman for a friendly dove. In the end, the dove, who has now taken the form of a tree, returns to his natural human form, that of a prince. The prince and young woman marry and live happily ever after.

D. An emperor is tricked into walking through the streets of his town naked by out-of-town tailors.

E. A prince is allowed to marry only the woman who can feel a single pea placed under numerous mattresses when she sleeps at the palace.

F. A woman's long hair saves her from life in a lonely tower when her hero climbs her locks to rescue her.

G. A poor little girl burns the matches she is supposed to sell in order to keep warm in this classic Christmas story.

H. A girl no bigger than a thimble marries a fairy prince in this tale.

I. A baby water fowl is mistaken for a duckling in this tale until he develops into a beautiful swan.

J. A girl and boy who have been enticed into the home of a wicked witch by the candy with which the house has been constructed save themselves by burning the witch

Name ______________________

From Fact to Fairy Tale

The stories of Hans Christian Andersen are full of irony, sarcasm, social commentary, and basic human truths. They are also full of disguised details, emotions, and events from Mr. Andersen's own life. Read the Andersen story plots below and tell what might have happened in his life to prompt each story. Write your responses in complete sentences.

"Children's Prattle" is a story about children from wealthy families who discuss their futures at a birthday party. One speaks of the requirement of having a solid family name in finding future success. Another speaks of the need for inherited money in making it big in the adult world. The third suggests only well-educated people are the ones who go far. At the end of the story, it is the poor and uneducated son of the cook at the party who becomes the most successful of all.
What might have happened in Andersen's life to prompt the writing of this story?

____

____

____

"The Saucy Boy" is the story of a young child who disguises himself in order to get close enough to shoot people in the heart with an arrow. The young boy, who is named Cupid, hits children, young adults, and even old people. The story's narrator calls the boy a nasty little thing.
What might have happened in Andersen's life to prompt the writing of this story?

____

____

____

"Little Ida's Flowers" tells about a boy who loves to cut out paper images and tell fantastic stories. He tells a girl named Ida about flowers that dance. Some people do not like the boy's tall tales, but Ida smiles as he talks. Eventually, she even begins to see dancing flowers herself.
What might have happened in Andersen's life to prompt the writing of this story?

____

____

____

"The Gardener and the Fine Family" relates the story of a family who appreciates anything that comes from a foreign land, but neglects to appreciate the fine produce that comes from the fields cultivated on their own land by their own gardener.
What might have happened in Andersen's life to prompt the writing of this story?

____

____

____

Name ______________________________

Light Tale, Deep Truths

Hans Christian Andersen did not set out to be a fairy-tale writer. He enjoyed writing novels, poems, travel stories, and plays just as much as he did fairy tales. Yet his fairy tales are what became classics because they so gracefully mix simple, childlike storylines with profound social commentaries and universal truths. In so doing, Hans Christian Andersen fairy tales entertain children while teaching moral lessons to their parents as well.

Choose one of the moral lessons or social comments listed below. Attempt to teach it by developing it into a complete fairy tale in the space provided.

Choice One: Teach the readers of your fairy tale that cheaters never prosper.
Choice Two: Convince the readers of your fairy tale that people today are too busy.
Choice Three: Convince the readers of your fairy tale that it is good to stand up for what you believe in.
Choice Four: Suggest to the readers of your fairy tale that people of all races and classes are equals.
Choice Five: Teach the readers of your fairy tale that it pays to be prepared.

Your Fairy Tale

Unwelcome Sleuth Success

Background

From 1837 until 1901, Queen Victoria reigned in England, Scotland, and Ireland, as well as in the new British colonial settlements of India, Canada, Australia, New Zealand, and South Africa. Times were good for Great Britain. Trade unions thrived. Working-class living standards were high. The telegraph made communications instant. Transportation infrastructure including roads and steamship routes expanded considerably. British entrepreneurs made fortunes building railroads during what would come to be known as the "Railway Age." British exports tripled with Victoria at the throne, and overseas investments quadrupled. Britain claimed the position of the greatest power in the newly industrialized world. Britain's naval supremacy assured the empire's safety for an unprecedented period of a hundred years. Art and architecture flourished in British cities. Literature and philosophy enjoyed center stage within high-society circles. Countless schools were established to educate the children of a rapidly growing middle class, and a national system of education was put into place. Parliament enjoyed a period of meaningful reform. Evangelical religions experienced a revival in numbers and sentiment, while diverting religious views enjoyed a period of tolerance. Queen Victoria and her husband Prince Albert encouraged and exemplified attitudes favoring family values, morality, and a sense of duty and respectability. The Victorian period was the Golden Age of Great Britain.

At this high moment of British glory, there arrived a civilized and rational fictional hero via *Strand* magazine. His cool reason and eloquent class instantly pleased not only literate Englishmen, but also readers as far away as New York. That is because Sherlock Holmes embodied Victorian England. He resided at a true address in London. He valued both art and reason. He displayed impeccable courage and civility as he encountered intriguing adventures set in the magnificent glory of his day. At the turn of the century, all of Great Britain—and a good deal of the rest of the world—was enamored with the ultimate gumshoe, Sherlock Holmes.

Only one man was less than impressed with the adventures of Mr. Holmes and his sidekick Watson. That man was the author of the Holmes' adventures, Sir Arthur Conan Doyle. In this lesson students read how a near-bankrupt eye doctor reached success in literature only to be immortalized as the creator of his own least favorite character.

Teaching Activities

Detecting Truths: Students use logic to help determine the truth of presented statements.
Doyle Contemporaries: Students learn about other famous authors of the Victorian era.

Extensions

1. Require students to write their own mysteries.
2. Require students to read and report on famous Sherlock Holmes stories.
3. Locate lesser-known Sir Arthur Conan Doyle stories on the Internet or in a library. Require students to read sections of the lesser-known work and to report on its similarities with and differences from the Sherlock Holmes stories.
4. Research and report on the history of ophthalmology. When Doyle was an eye doctor, what methods were being used to test and treat patients?

Student Reading

Unwelcome Sleuth Success

From 1876 until 1881 a young man named Arthur Conan Doyle studied medicine at Scotland's Edinburgh University, working as a doctor's assistant between terms to pay for his schooling. Upon his graduation, the young man accepted a short-term position as medic on a ship bound for West Africa. Then in September 1882 Dr. Doyle finally got to practice his specialty of ophthalmology. Yet his practice did not keep him busy nor make him rich.

In a day before insurance, medical doctors who wanted to make a good living either had to see an exorbitant number of patients or cater to a wealthy clientele. Dr. Doyle did neither. So, to supplement his mediocre eye-doctoring income and to pass the time between patient visits, the young man sat down at the desk in his medical office and tried his hand at writing.

Alas, the articles he wrote for medical journals and the short stories he contributed to popular magazines did little to add to the wealth of the young doctor who was attempting to support a growing family. Even the fascinating story of intrigue written with one of Doyle's ingeniously deductive Edinburgh teachers in mind failed to bring in many dollars—or catch the attention of many readers, for that matter.

"A Study in Scarlet" did, however, catch the attention of George Newnes. The highly respected publisher was preparing to launch a new magazine aimed at London business people when he ran into Dr. Doyle at a dinner party. Newnes said that if Doyle would care to write a complete series of self-contained short stories about this Sherlock Holmes who was featured in "A Study in Scarlet," *Strand* magazine would publish them at the rate of one per monthly issue.

Arthur Conan Doyle readily accepted the terms. After all, he had just returned from Vienna and Paris where he had gained the latest knowledge about eye diseases but earned absolutely no income. He could easily write 12 short stories between April and November of 1891 in between patient visits if he were able to use the same setting and characters for each story. And so he did.

By December of 1892 Arthur Doyle, the struggling optician, found that he had become Arthur Doyle, the wealthy author. Sherlock Holmes stories were immensely popular with the public—not only in England, but in the United States as well. Magazines in New York bought Doyle's stories from *Strand* to run in their monthly publications, and publishers on both sides of the Atlantic soon bound the entire set of stories into best-selling books.

George Newnes expectedly asked Doyle to write another year's worth of Sherlock Holmes stories. Doyle unexpectedly tried to dissuade him. Although Dr. Doyle loved to write, he found the detective story to be tiresome and second-rate. Doyle enjoyed writing medieval romances, science fiction, political essays, and works on spirituality. So, he told Newnes he would continue the Holmes series only if he were paid 1,000 pounds for the next 12 stories. Doyle had attempted to quote a figure so high (the modern-day equivalent of about two years' middle-class salary) that Newnes would reject his terms. Newnes surprised Doyle. He agreed to the offer and sent Doyle back to the writing desk to set Sherlock Holmes back to detective work again.

In December 1893 the public was presented with what was to be the final story of Sherlock Holmes. "The Final Problem" ended with the good detective dead in the arms of his archenemy, Professor Moriarty. Arthur Conan Doyle was relieved to see the demise of his famed character. Now he could return to the medical practice he had completely abandoned, spend time with his family, serve as a physician and correspondent in the Boer War, receive the honor of knighthood for his public support of the British military, and direct his literary talent to the writing of historical novels, political essays, and spiritual studies.

The English and American public was not happy to see the demise of Sherlock Holmes. In fact, everyone from Doyle's own mother to Queen Victoria demanded he be brought back to life. Finally, ten years after the publication of "The Final Problem," Doyle relented. In 1903 he quite rationally explained away what only appeared to be the death of Holmes in the story of a decade before, and went on to write what were to be combined into a volume titled *The Return of Sherlock Holmes.*

All counted, Doyle wrote 68 Sherlock Holmes tales in addition to his other works, which he considered more significant. He popularized the detective genre and brought to life a character whose image continues to be more recognizable than any except distinct religious symbols worldwide. Sales and translations of Sherlock Holmes stories are second only to those of the Bible all across the globe. The character who would not die in 1893, will not die today. Sir Arthur Conan Doyle may have been a fine doctor, exceptional author of science fiction, motivational speaker on the topic of spirituality, and beloved husband and father, but to the world, he will forever be the creator of Mr. Sherlock Holmes, brilliantly deductive super sleuth.

Name ______________________________

Detecting Truths

Using deductive reasoning, determine whether the statements following each paragraph below are true or false. Explain the reasoning behind your guesses in the spaces provided. The first one has been done for you as an example.

1. The detective genre was born in 1841. Sir Arthur Conan Doyle did not write his first story featuring Sherlock Holmes until 1887. "The Mystery of the Sassana Valley," which he wrote two years prior to 1887, was also a detective tale.
   TRUE or FALSE: *Sir Arthur Conan Doyle invented the detective story.*
   REASONING: Doyle's first detective story was written 44 years after the genre was born.
2. The first detective story ever written was titled "The Murders in the Rue Morgue." "The Murders in the Rue Morgue" was written by Edgar Allan Poe.
   TRUE or FALSE: Edgar Allan Poe is considered the "Father of the Detective Story."
   REASONING: ______________________________

   ____
3. In the mid-1800s Edgar Allan Poe assigned murder cases to a pipe-smoking, logical character named C. Auguste Dupin in several short stories that were narrated by a nameless friend of the detective. In 1868 Wilkie Collins published a novel in which a detective aids a less-competent policeman in solving a case of a stolen jewel.
   TRUE or FALSE: Sir Arthur Conan Doyle borrowed ideas from previous authors in establishing the premise of his Sherlock Holmes stories.
   REASONING: ______________________________

   ____
4. The character of Sherlock Holmes was fashioned after a professor at the medical school of Edinburgh University who had the uncanny ability to diagnose patients before listening to their symptoms. Holmes' name reflects Doyle's appreciation for the poetry of Oliver Wendell Holmes. Just as was Doyle himself, Holmes' sidekick was a medical doctor with few patients. Dr. Watson was named after a friend of Doyle who was the president of the Portsmouth Literary and Philosophical Society. The scenes in Sherlock Holmes stories reflected closely Victorian life in England. Holmes and Watson worked and resided at 221B Baker Street, an actual address in London.
   TRUE or FALSE: Arthur Conan Doyle imagined the world of Sherlock Holmes without consideration for the actual world around him.
   REASONING: ______________________________

   ____
5. Sir Arthur Conan Doyle enjoyed boxing and motorcar racing. He played football and cricket on national teams. He once acted as an "unofficial diplomat" to Africa. He spoke in support of law reform in England. He wrote books and spoke out on the topic of spirituality. He served as a medical doctor on ships, in war, and in a private practice. He married twice (his first wife died) and fathered five children.
   TRUE or FALSE: Sir Arthur Conan Doyle wrote short stories at such a feverish rate that his entire life revolved around literary pursuits.
   REASONING: ______________________________

   ____

Name ______________________________

Doyle Contemporaries

The era in which Sir Arthur Conan Doyle wrote stories was a golden age in English literature. Use an encyclopedia or reference book to help you match the other famous British authors from the Victorian era with their descriptions below.

JAMES JOYCE	LEWIS CARROLL	LORD ALFRED TENNYSON
RUDYARD KIPLING	D. H. LAWRENCE	GEORGE ELIOT
H. G. WELLS	VIRGINIA WOOLF	CHARLES DICKENS
		ELIZABETH BARRETT BROWNING

__________________ 1. This Englishman who was born in India became the first British winner of the Nobel Prize for Literature in 1907. He was immensely popular in his own day for such short story collections as *Plain Tales from the Hills* and continues to be popular today for such children's works as the *Just So Stories.*

__________________ 2. This Irish poet and novelist used the stream-of-consciousness technique to write such timeless classics as *Ulysses.*

__________________ 3. Many of the works of this English author of the classics *Women in Love* and *Lady Chatterley's Lover* reflected his working-class background.

__________________ 4. This late nineteenth-century English poet was immensely popular in her own day for works including *Sonnets from the Portuguese,* but her accomplishments have been overshadowed today by those of her now-famous husband, Robert.

__________________ 5. This English author who struggled with depression her entire life until finally committing suicide wrote brilliant criticisms and stream-of-consciousness style novels.

__________________ 6. This popular English writer was appointed Poet Laureate by Queen Victoria in 1850.

__________________ 7. This greatest of English novelists, renowned for his socially conscious classics including *Oliver Twist* and *David Copperfield,* often drew from his childhood memories of debtor's prison and factory work.

__________________ 8. This author of the *Mill on the Floss* wrote under a pseudonym so that book publishers would not guess that she was a woman.

__________________ 9. This British writer and social reformer is remembered for classic works of science fiction including *The Time Machine* and *The War of the Worlds.*

__________________ 10. This English mathematician became famous not only for his brilliant mathematical treaties but also for his fanciful children's stories including *Alice in Wonderland.*

The World Is My Home

Background

An epic is a majestic, broad-sweeping narrative literary work dealing with historic or legendary events of a single nation or people. Rather than focusing on the personality traits of individual characters, epics express the ideals and traditions of an entire culture or religion. Most often, epics are composed long after the conclusion of the events that inspired their creation; therefore, they draw substantially on folklore and folk songs. Great literary epic classics include Virgil's first-century B.C. *Aeneid*, Homer's eighth-century *Iliad*, Dante's fourteenth-century *The Divine Comedy*, and John Milton's 1667 *Paradise Lost*.

Traditionally, epics have been written in the form of narrative poems. Even as the nineteenth century witnessed revisions in traditional epic styles including a move toward more personalized themes and more prose-like verse, epics continued to be poems. Equally traditional has been the practice of the writing of epics from within the culture, nation, or religion they describe. Native Greeks have written about Greece. Christian humanists have written about the humanist movement in Christianity.

James A. Michener turned the tables on tradition. In 1959 the already Pulitzer Prize-winning author wrote a long fictional saga in prose that incorporated stories, cultural realities, and folklore of the people of Hawaii. Michener was not a native of Hawaii, and his work was not a narrative poem, but his approximately 900-page majestic narrative earned the "epic" label. It also earned blockbuster status. Overnight, James A. Michener was a phenomenal, best-selling author with an eager following who excitedly anticipated his next works. With impeccable historical accuracy, cultural respect beyond compare, and a keen eye for the universal human condition, Mr. Michener went on to write 40 critically acclaimed epics that delivered whole states and whole nations to 75 million anxious readers who devoured page after page of his long, meandering tales.

In this lesson students learn how an extremely poor orphan child grew into a skilled athlete who became a respected educator who marched off to war and returned home with a Pulitzer Prize-winning novel scribbled on the backs of letters from home.

Teaching Activities

Panoramic Views: Students try their hand at writing setting descriptions Michener style.
Name That Epic: Students identify Michener titles by reading descriptions of his works.

Extensions

1. Assign the writing of an epic tale about the history, folklore, and traditions of your school or community.
2. Assign the writing of sagas based on the extended families of your students.
3. Read aloud to your students portions of James Michener's works.
4. Assign individual or group reports on some of the places Michener wrote about including Texas, Alaska, South Africa, Hawaii, and outer space.
5. Require students to draw or paint scenery based on Michener descriptions.
6. Research and report on the history of the Pulitzer Prize. Assign reports on other Pulitzer Prize-winning novelists.
7. Read famous epic poems with your class. Compare and contrast epic narrative poems with narrative epic prose.

The World Is My Home

In 1931 a recent graduate of New England's Swarthmore College won the Joshua Lippincott Fellowship, which allowed its recipient to travel and study in Europe for two years. The young winner made the very most of his prize. In addition to attending classes at St. Andrews School in Scotland, he toured with Spanish bullfighters, studied art in major European cities, worked on a Mediterranean cargo ship, and collected folk legends in the Hebrides Islands off the coast of Scotland.

On February 3, 1907, James was born probably in the city of New York, to a mother who chose not to keep her child. A poor Quaker widow, who took in laundry and sewing jobs in an attempt to provide for the two children she already had, rescued the abandoned infant and raised him as her own in nearby Doylestown, Pennsylvania. Michener was the poorest student in Doylestown's school system. He wore worn out sneakers in the middle of winter and ragged clothing year round. On several occasions, Mr. Michener recalled his mother leaving him and his siblings in the care of the local poorhouse for weeks at a time so she could be certain her children would be fed three meals a day.

James Michener was not bowed by his early experiences. He reported in later life that he felt no jealousy or sadness in childhood when other children received Christmas presents and he did not. Monetary things simply meant nothing to him. James knew he was an exceptional student and an outstanding athlete, and that was enough. In fact, Michener even suggested in later life that playing on a consistently winning basketball team in high school made him feel like such a champion that he absolutely knew he would make something big of his adult life.

He just did not know exactly what—for 40 years. Following his time in Europe in the early 1930s, Michener returned to the states as a teacher of social studies at a Quaker school in Bucks County, Pennsylvania. From 1936 until 1939, he worked and studied at the Colorado State College of Education, where he earned his master's degree and served as an associate professor. From 1939 until 1940, Michener taught at Harvard's Graduate School of Education as a visiting lecturer while finding time to write two scholarly volumes on the current and future states of social studies education. It seemed James Michener would make his mark in the field of education.

Then in 1940, Michener was hired by Macmillan Publishing Company in the capacity of social studies editor. It was again a position in the field of education, but Michener later recalled that it was at Macmillan that he "learned what a great many people never learn . . . how to write a sentence and how to write a paragraph." A stubborn and determined effort to do just that over and over again every day of the remaining years of his life, coupled with Michener's insatiable curiosity about the world at large, led to the former high school basketball champion's crowning victory in adulthood.

At the height of World War II, Michener was sent to the South Pacific as a new enlistee in the Naval Reserves. During his three years in the service, he worked his way up to the rank of lieutenant commander and served as the Navy's South Pacific naval historian. In that position, Lt. Commander Michener spent more than two years hopping from island to island taking in the scenery, marveling at the culture, and soaking up the stories of experience and folklore recited by natives and fellow soldiers alike. Everything James Michener learned, he wrote down—not only on the official forms of the South Pacific naval historian—but also on the backs of envelopes and open spaces of letters from home. James Michener had the notion that South Pacific living was filling other soldiers with the same vivid and invigorating sensations that he was experiencing. He was banking on the prediction that once the men returned home, they would enjoy reading about their glorious time spent on the islands and at sea.

As soon as he returned to the states, James Michener prepared his makeshift manuscript for publication. In 1947, the year Michener celebrated his fortieth birthday, *Tales of the South Pacific* was published and released to book stores nationwide. Its initial commercial success was minimal, but Michener's first novel earned him the 1948 Pulitzer Prize for fiction. Rodgers and Hammerstein turned the short stories from the book into a phenomenally successful Broadway musical. The book sold more copies. Between the royalties gained from the Broadway show and the sales of the book itself, James Michener suddenly found himself in the financial position to direct all of his attention to writing.

During the next 11 years, Michener cranked out ten more works before striking gold again. In 1959 Michener presented the world with the first of his epic 900-page novels that related the history, botany, geography, and culture of an entire region in such a readable format to make his monumental works blockbusters. *Hawaii* became an instant success. Six years later *The Source* repeated the accomplishment. By the time of his death in 1997, Michener had written rich tapestries of the history and cultures of a dozen places including Texas, South Africa, Israel, Spain, Poland, the American West, the South Pacific, Alaska, the Caribbean, and even outer space.

No matter what the topic, Michener fans purchased his latest masterpiece for nearly 40 years, knowing that they would be treated to nearly a thousand pages of fiction set in the most accurate of historical, cultural, and geographic settings. Michener books sold nearly one hundred million copies. Movies, plays, and television miniseries tackled Michener's stories in the performing arts. Translations of Michener's 47 books have been written in more than 50 languages. James Michener made enough money off the sales of his books that he was able to donate a total of over $100 million dollars to various colleges, museums, and libraries. Michener's remarkable knowledge of varied topics from politics to botany earned him honorary degrees in five different subject areas at over 30 institutions. His intelligence and abilities also earned him a seat on numerous presidential advisory boards, a position as correspondent during President Nixon's trip to China and Russia, and the honor of receiving a Medal of Freedom from President Ford. The boy who started out life claimed by one widowed woman grew into a man admired by the world.

Name ____________________

Panoramic Views

James Michener vividly described settings both to paint a clear picture of a physical place and to invoke the spirit of a place. Read the two Michener passages below and then try your own hand at descriptive writing for each of his two purposes. An example has been done for you.

Describing to Define a Physical Setting: "Coconut palms nodding gracefully toward the ocean . . . Reefs upon which waves broke into spray, inner lagoons . . . the sweating jungle, the full moon rising behind the volcanoes." (from *Tales of the South Pacific*)
Describing to Invoke the Spirit of a Place: "Do not come to these islands empty-handed, or craven in spirit, or afraid to starve. There is no food here. In these islands there is no certainty . . . But if you come with growing things, and good foods, and better ideas . . . if you are willing to do work . . . then you can gain entrance to this miraculous crucible . . . On these harsh terms the island waits." (from *Hawaii*)

1A. Define the physical setting of your bedroom: School books lie open, balancing atop crumpled T-shirts and candy bar wrappers. Paper and pencils and pens and erasers cover the desk, the bed, and the top of the television set. Empty pop cans and discarded peanut shells crunch under the feet of any who dare to enter my room.

1B. Invoke the spirit of your bedroom: The clutter of my personal cave calls out to the creative. Should one who enters my room have an instant brainstorm, a pen and paper are easily at hand. Should one feel inspired to study for a school test, he will find a book already open on my floor. Should one wonder what week-old popcorn or the final swig at the bottom of a ten-day-old bottle of pop should taste like, he can test his hypotheses without leaving my room. It may be unorganized—even a bit of a mess—but my bedroom defines my creativity, my ongoing experiment with life.

2A. Describe the physical setting of a ballpark: ____________________

____

____

2B. Invoke the spirit of a ballpark: ____________________

____

____

3A. Describe the physical setting of an amusement park: ____________________

____

____

3B. Invoke the spirit of an amusement park: ____________________

____

____

4A. Describe the physical setting of a courtroom: ____________________

____

____

4B. Invoke the spirit of a courtroom: ____________________

____

____

Name ______________________________

Name That Epic

James A. Michener did not hide the themes of his epic narratives behind obscure titles. Identify each of the following self-evident Michener titles by its description.

DESCRIPTION

_____ 1. This extensive saga flashes back on 800 years of adventures in the lives of three families who, at the beginning of the novel, are engrossed in a clash between militant farmers and the Communist leaders who govern their nation.

_____ 2. This tapestry of the developing American West focuses on the conflicts between Native Americans and migrating white traders, homesteaders, and gold seekers.

_____ 3. This epic story spans seven centuries beginning with a description of the lush island of Dominica in 1310 and works its way through Columbus' arrival in the region, the establishment of Spanish control, the 1800 slave revolt in Haiti, and the rise of Castro to power in Cuba.

_____ 4. This story, set in the towns along the United States Eastern shoreline, is a 400-year saga that tells the story of the forming of a nation.

_____ 5. This novel explores the evils of drug abuse as it follows six runaways who are adrift in the worlds of Spain, Marrakech, and Mozambique.

_____ 6. This epic spans the history of Spain introducing readers to bullfighters, warrior kings, peasants, and artists while painting vivid pictures of olive orchards, orange groves, and elaborate cathedrals.

_____ 7. This mix of historic fact and fiction traces the source of Christianity from the early days of Hebrews and Jews through the Crusades and the Spanish Inquisition and on to the modern conflicts in Israel and the Middle East.

_____ 8. This fictional account of the lives of writers integrates many facts as do all of Michener's narratives.

TITLE

A. *Caribbean*

B. *Texas*

C. *Chesapeake*

D. *Iberia*

E. *Novel*

F. *Centennial*

G. *Drifters*

H. *The Source*

I. *Tales of the South Pacific*

J. *Mexico*

K. *Covenant*

L. *Space*

M. *Journey*

N. *Alaska*

O. *Poland*

P. *Hawaii*

_____ 9. In this epic of the land "south of the border," an American journalist gets swept into a story of the nation's history, forms a description of the days of its ancient natives to the times of invading Spaniards, and moves on to give an account of modern-day trials.

_____10. This story follows the lives of six men and women who have devoted their lives to the exploration of the "final frontier."

_____11. This first of Michener's narratives is the Pulitzer Prize-winning story of the interconnected lives of soldiers, natives, nurses, and sailors during World War II in a tropical paradise.

_____12. This epic of South Africa tells the story of the Bushmen, white invasion, and forced "covenant" of Apartheid across the panoramic description of a jungle nation full of wildlife and natural beauty.

_____13. This novel chronicles the journey of four aristocratic Englishmen and one Irish servant across Canada in their attempt to reach the riches of California gold.

_____14. This first popular Michener epic is the story of clashes between the simple traditions of the people who inhabit a group of quiet islands and the American missionaries who attempt to convert the natives away from their own established morals, customs, and religions.

_____15. This epic narrative is the story of natives and newcomers who attempt to survive against all odds in a majestic land of snow and ice.

_____16. This epic tale begins in the early 1500s with a description of native life, and works its way through the Spanish invasion and the political wheeling and dealing that turned this land into a state of this nation. In broad brush strokes, it explores the state's rise in cotton production and cattle ranching, and discusses the discovery of oil and the state's modern expansion in industry.

Acclaim and Controversy

Background

The close of the Civil War and the passage of the Thirteenth Amendment, which liberated slaves in this nation from bondage, did not suddenly result in a society governed by racial equality. Reconstruction legislation aimed at building an acceptable social order in the post-Civil War South met with intense opposition. A civil rights bill, which granted the privileges of citizenship to "all persons born in the United States regardless of race or color," was initially ignored and eventually revoked. Instead, Southern states passed Black Codes, which pigeonholed African American citizens into inferior social and economic status. In effect, many blacks were relegated to their former roles as farmhands in arrangements of sharecropping, which offered little advantage over the conditions of slavery.

Scare tactics were employed to prevent African Americans from voting, running for public office, or maintaining businesses in "white" sections of communities. State and city ordinances were used to segregate blacks from whites by prohibiting minorities from riding in "whites only" railroad cars, sitting in "whites only" sections of buses and restaurants, or drinking from "whites only" public drinking fountains.

Into the midst of this injustice that continued in the South for 100 years following the end of the Civil War, Alice Walker was born. The eighth and youngest child of poor sharecropping parents in Eatonton, Georgia, Alice Walker eventually overcame the injustices of her day to become a highly successful and critically acclaimed, albeit controversial, author. In this lesson students read how the depression and insecurity that followed a childhood accident prompted Alice Walker to write poetry and short stories that would eventually earn her fame, acclaim, and a degree of criticism.

Teaching Activities

On the Shoulders of Giants and **Walker Contemporaries:** Students study authors who influenced Alice Walker as well as the contributions of other African American authors of the twentieth century.

Extensions

1. Assign the reading of an age-appropriate Alice Walker novel to students.
2. Conduct a debate on the pros and cons of portraying African Americans in a bad light in literature as Alice Walker often does. Consider the viewpoints of both her critics and her supporters.
3. Research and report on the history of African Americans in the United States.
4. Assign the writing of a social commentary piece based on injustices students have witnessed in their own lives.
5. Assign reports on the Civil Rights Movement in which Alice Walker was active.
6. Require students to write about tragedies or mistakes in their own lives that result in positive experiences (such as Alice Walker's insecurities leading her to writing).

Acclaim and Controversy

Alice Walker understands pain. Most minorities born into the segregated world of the American South during the first half of the twentieth century understand pain. During the decades prior to the passage of the Civil Rights Act of 1964, African Americans were subjected to the cruelty and injustice of frequently spoken racial slurs; segregated public accommodations; legally overlooked lynchings of socially critical friends and neighbors; and inferior employment, educational, and housing opportunities. Alice Walker was subjected to additional hardships.

Alice Walker was the eighth child of poor sharecroppers who lived in a cramped Eatonton, Georgia, shack with a leaking roof. At the age of eight, she was playing a game of "cowboys and Indians" with her brothers when a BB gun pellet struck her in the right eye. The accident left Alice with not only blindness in her right eye, but also a conspicuous scar on her cornea. The white scar tissue in her eye embarrassed Alice. The formerly outgoing child became quiet and withdrawn. When thoughtless children made fun of her scar, she cried. When caring people attempted to engage Alice in conversation, she bowed her head so they could not look her in the eye. When Alice's parents sent Alice to live with her grandmother in hopes that a new start would bring her renewed happiness, she misinterpreted the decision as a punishment for becoming ugly. For the first of many times in her challenging life, Alice Walker turned to reading and writing for solace.

Surgery eventually removed the scar tissue from Walker's eye, and the Civil Rights Movement eventually lifted many of the restrictions placed on this nation's minorities, but Walker never forgot the feelings of shame and hurt she experienced in her youth. Indeed, she has dedicated her adult life to the righting of wrongs. When Martin Luther King, Jr., asked for people to march to Washington, D.C., in protest of segregation laws in the South, Alice Walker answered the call. When Helsinki, Finland, hosted an international Youth World Peace Festival, Alice Walker volunteered to represent her region. In the early 1960s, Walker joined other college students in the South in conducting sit-ins wherein minorities ignored the "Whites Only" signs in public establishments. Later she walked door to door in an effort to register black voters who had been scared away from voter registration booths by white political leaders. When Sarah Lawrence College in New York offered Alice Walker a scholarship with the warning that she would be one of a very few minority students attending the school, she accepted the challenge. Upon graduating from college, Walker accepted a job working in the welfare department of New York City and later in a Head Start program in Mississippi. When a white, Jewish man asked for her hand in marriage, she accepted the offer to become one half of the first legally recognized interracial marriage in Mississippi. Before even reaching the age of 25, Walker had participated in numerous demonstrations, accepted an invitation to dinner at the home of Martin Luther King, Jr., and traveled to both Europe and Africa, where she gained an appreciation for the world's varied cultures.

Still, Walker's private life was far from perfect, as were the lives of many African American women. In response to personal struggles, at the age of 20 Walker returned to her childhood comfort of writing. In response to her belief that many African American women do not get treated kindly by their spouses and boyfriends, she turned to writing again.

Immediately upon publication at the urging of her mentor Muriel Ruykeyser at Sarah Lawrence University, the works of Alice Walker were recognized as much more than therapeutic writings. Langston Hughes praised Walker's first short story, and writing fellowship committees around the country awarded her funds to continue her work. Over the course of the next ten years, Walker wrote novels, short stories, and poems while also teaching at colleges and editing the magazine *Ms.* Both aspects of her life were successful. While teaching at Wellesley College, Walker offered one of the nation's first women's studies courses, hers focusing on the contributions of African American women writers. With nearly each newly published writing, Walker accepted another literary award.

Then in 1982 Walker's novel *The Color Purple* was published. The work received the American Book Award of the year and a 1982 Pulitzer Prize. The novel's storyline was adapted into a Hollywood movie. Suddenly, the writings of Alice Walker were world famous. They were also highly controversial. Many African Americans accused Walker of treating her black male characters too harshly. Critics said a literary statement that many black men do not treat their wives and girlfriends kindly would be detrimental to the ongoing movement for racial equality in the nation.

Alice Walker disagrees. She believes shedding light on all injustices equally will ultimately free the oppressed. Remembering her childhood feelings of shame and inferiority as a disfigured, visually impaired little black girl in the segregated South, Alice Walker continues to write to bring comfort and healing both to herself, and now to millions of fans worldwide.

Name ______________________________

On the Shoulders of Giants

Alice Walker did a great deal of reading following her "cowboys and Indians" accident in 1952. Later she both studied and taught about great authors in college as a student and professor.

Use outside resources to help you identify by description the following writers who influenced Alice Walker.

WILLIAM FAULKNER	BESSIE HEAD	EMILY DICKINSON
LEO TOLSTOY	GWENDOLYN BROOKS	ALBERT CAMUS
FYODOR DOSTOEVSKY	E. E. CUMMINGS	DORIS LESSING
THE BRONTË SISTERS		

_______________ 1. This nineteenth-century, American poet lived in seclusion and wrote lyrical verse about immortality and nature. Her works did not become recognized until after her death in 1886.

_______________ 2. This classic Russian author of the masterpiece *War and Peace* is renowned not only for his flawless and flowing writing style, but also for his psychologically complete portrayal of characters.

_______________ 3. This British author of *The Golden Notebook*, who grew up in Southern Rhodesia, is known for her writings about women's issues.

_______________ 4. These prolific sisters contributed to English literature such classics as *Jane Eyre* and *Wuthering Heights*.

_______________ 5. This United States poet of the early twentieth century became famous for his unconventional use of punctuation, typography, and language.

_______________ 6. This Noble and Pulitzer Prize-winning American novelist is known for his complex novels and short stories dealing with the death of the Old South.

_______________ 7. This classic Russian novelist who dealt with the subjects of sin and suffering, suffered a great deal himself. He spent four years of hard labor in Siberia as a political prisoner; he watched his brother and his wife die of illness; and he endured the lifelong ailment of epilepsy.

_______________ 8. This French playwright and essayist conveyed through his works his philosophical belief that humans would get along best in life if they would admit the absurdities of the entire universe.

_______________ 9. This American poet, who became known for her short verse-line poems depicting the struggles of black citizens, became the first African American to win a Pulitzer Prize.

_______________ 10. Best known for her novel *A Question of Power*, this South African author dealt with issues of good and evil in the world of apartheid.

Name ______________________

Walker Contemporaries

Alice Walker is one of several African American authors who rose to fame during the twentieth century. Use a dictionary to help you identify her contemporaries listed below.

LANGSTON HUGHES	RICHARD WRIGHT	JAMES BALDWIN
TONI MORRISON	RALPH ELLISON	ZORA NEALE HURSTON
MAYA ANGELOU		

______________ 1. This author of *Invisible Man* contends that American society intentionally ignores African Americans.

______________ 2. This prolific author of such works as *Uncle Tom's Children* and *Native Son* insisted on making the problems of prejudice and racial injustice public.

______________ 3. This versatile individual greatly influenced Harlem Renaissance writers as she wrote fiction, collected and wrote folktales, and completed anthropological research on her racial heritage.

______________ 4. This American poet of the Harlem Renaissance period adapted the rhythms of African American music to his classic poems.

______________ 5. This famous novelist and essayist insisted in such writings as *Tell Me How Long the Train's Been Gone* that the conflicts blacks experienced in America are symbolic of conflict in general.

______________ 6. Drawing on the experiences of a rich and painful past, this author contributed the classic *I Know Why the Caged Bird Sings* to American literature.

______________ 7. This Nobel Prize-winning author of *Beloved* writes rich and complex stories of the black experience in America.

Now choose an author from this or the preceding page to study in depth. Write a brief summary of the author's life and works below, and draw or glue a copy of an illustration or photograph of the author in the box provided.

A "Paine"ful Life

Background

By January of 1776, the American Revolution had been in progress for nine full months. Still militia men were not fighting for the independence of a new nation. Along with most other Americans, the colonial soldiers hoped that their skirmishes with British troops would force the hand of King George III into meeting some of the demands of the Declaration of Rights and Grievances that was presented to him in 1774. They did not expect to sever relations with Britain, but to improve them.

Yet the tide of public opinion was turning. Under their breath, colonists were whispering concerns that relations could not be improved. America was growing up. It once relied on immigrants from England to help build an infrastructure and establish new villages. It depended on the stability of the British crown to give a semblance of law in a new land. By the late eighteenth century, America no longer needed Britain's assistance. In fact, Britain was rather in the way. American colonies had legal documents of their own. Their towns were populated. Their infrastructures were up and running. Their farms were yielding crops. British taxes, troops, and governors were now standing in the way of progress.

So America entered its teenage stage. The finest statesmen gathered at the First Continental Congress and devised the Declaration of Rights and Grievances. It was not a cry for independence. It was simply a plea for looser chains. American colonies no longer required the direction of British governors. American colonists did not want to pay taxes to a motherland that did not even allow her child representation in parliament. American colonists did not want to have to conduct all major official business 3,000 miles from their doorstep. America wanted elbow room to grow up.

Originally, to most citizens, this meant demanding reform—either through documents or battles. To Thomas Paine it meant breaking free. The January 1776 pamphlet Mr. Paine wrote entitled *Common Sense* maintained, "It is repugnant to reason . . . to suppose, that this continent can longer remain subject to any external power." Thomas Paine was ready to witness the birth of a new nation, and the American colonists quickly agreed. Paine sold 500,000 copies of his pamphlet—one to every four citizens in the nation. Within six months, the Second Continental Congress was convening to draw up a new document—the Declaration of Independence. In 1776 Thomas Paine was raised to the shoulders of a brand new nation. In 1792 he was lowered back to the ground. It would be more than a century before he claimed his rightful place in American history again.

In this lesson students read about the cycle of highs and lows in the life of a man who insisted on speaking his mind!

Teaching Activities

Paine Talk: Students distinguish among quotes from famous Thomas Paine documents.
Fightin' Words: Students discuss times when it is appropriate to speak your mind, even if your words might be unpopular.

Extensions

1. Locate original Thomas Paine works in a library or on the Internet and study full texts or excerpts with your students.
2. Assign reports on other famous leaders of the American Revolutionary movement.
3. Create a time line of events leading up to the writing of the Declaration of Independence.

A "Paine"ful Life

Thomas Paine once said, "Reputation is what men and women think of us; character is what God and the angels know of us." Hopefully, Mr. Paine valued the opinions of God and angels over those of men and women, because men and women were not always kind to Thomas Paine.

The life of Thomas Paine did not begin with failures that eventually transformed into successes. The life of Thomas Paine consisted of many ups and downs. It began on the down side in a small town about 100 miles from London. Paine gained only a simple education before dropping out of school at the age of 13 to help his father manufacture whalebone corsets. When that proved unsatisfying, he ran away to sea. His sailor days lasted only a few years. Then he returned home to a position as a tax collector. When he published a pamphlet suggesting that better wages paid to government workers would curb corruption, Paine found himself looking for yet another job. For awhile he labored as a teacher, a tobacconist, and then a writer. It was in that last position that he met Benjamin Franklin while patronizing a London coffeehouse.

Benjamin Franklin liked Thomas Paine and helped his life take one of its many upturns. Franklin provided Paine with a letter of recommendation and suggested he find employment in the New World. Paine followed Franklin's advice. In 1774 he moved to America and began editing the *Pennsylvania Magazine*. A step ahead of his time, Paine published articles opposing slavery and advocating the rights of women and the elderly, the decent treatment of animals, and the need for universal and free education. He also stirred up the hearts of men and women who were already battling the British by authoring a document entitled *Common Sense* in which he suggested, "The birthday of a new world is at hand." In six months' time, the Declaration of Independence was presented to King George and a new nation was indeed born. Thomas Paine was an American hero. Every fourth citizen of the new country owned a copy of *Common Sense*. Some noted a marked similarity between its text and that of the Declaration. Some modern historians have even suggested that Thomas Paine did more than prompt the writing of the Declaration of Independence—that he actually authored the first draft.

Yet even with the drafting of the document, the revolution was far from over, and soldiers became discouraged at the odds of triumphing over such a great and established power as Britain. Even George Washington bemoaned in a letter to a friend, ". . . the history of this war is a history of false hopes . . . our efforts are in vain."

Thomas Paine disagreed. He enlisted in the Continental Army and turned once again to the power of the pen. He authored 13 papers, collectively called *The American Crisis*, which encouraged his fellow revolutionaries to such a degree that George Washington insisted they be read to all of the troops. "These are the times that try men's souls," Paine began his first document, scribbling on a drumhead at a battleside campfire, ". . . but he that stands it now deserves the love and thanks of man and woman."

When words were not enough, Paine turned to fund-raising. Relying on his own funds, which were meager since he donated moneys earned from *Common Sense* to the Continental Congress, Paine traveled to France where he secured a shipload of provisions from the government.

Thomas Paine had helped initiate the fight for independence, and he had helped it succeed. The Pennsylvania Assembly granted Paine a few thousand dollars. The state of New York presented him with the deed to a confiscated Loyalist farm in New Rochelle. Paine put down the pen for awhile and began working on a single-arch bridge design. At Ben Franklin's suggestion once again, he moved to Paris to be close to the French Academy of Sciences, an institution that might consider building his bridge. Once his bridge was built, he found himself in another land about to embark on revolution. Again he turned to his pen.

While visiting London, Thomas Paine wrote a stinging criticism of monarchies in *The Rights of Man* that earned him an accusation of treason from the British government. The French, however, in the midst of their revolution, were impressed. The new democracy in that land granted Thomas Paine immediate citizenship. Four separate districts elected him to the new National Assembly. Thomas Paine assisted in the writing of both the French Declaration of the Rights of Man and the Constitution of France. Alas, his fame was short-lived in his new home.

In a speech before the assembly, Mr. Paine suggested the king not be killed, but rather exiled. "My language has always been that of liberty and humanity," he said. "Kill the King, but not the man." This time his words gained Thomas Paine a place on death row. Only a chance error in the marking of death row prison cells, a later turn of events in the revolution, and a change in American ambassadors to France saved the life of Thomas Paine.

While in prison, he wrote yet another personal statement of beliefs. *The Age of Reason* discussed his religious views. It contended that faith in God was not something that could be boiled down to a few religious ceremonies. Going to church was not living by faith; promoting justice, mercy, and happiness among fellow creatures was living by faith. His ideas are not terribly shocking today, but they did not go over well in 1795.

Although he procured passage back to the United States with the help of President Thomas Jefferson, he did not arrive to any ticker tape parades. His fellow Americans considered Paine an atheist. A smear campaign ensued in which lies about his mannerisms, personality traits, and character suggested Thomas Paine was an unclean lying, cheating, God-hating drunkard. When he died in 1809, he was an infamous pauper. Only his housekeeper, her children, two black men, and a Quaker woman attended his funeral. The obituary in a June 8, 1809, New York City newspaper read, "He had lived long, did some good and much harm." One hundred years after his passing, President Theodore Roosevelt referred to Thomas Paine in a public interview as a "dirty little atheist." Thankfully, today's history books remember Thomas Paine as the brave and intelligent spokesperson for justice and freedom that he was.

Name ______________________________

Paine Talk

See if you can identify which Thomas Paine quotes first appeared in these documents based on the descriptions of the documents' purposes provided. Indicate your responses by writing the document title of your choice in the space provided before each quotation.

Common Sense was a pamphlet written anonymously which asserted that America was ready to stand alone, as its own nation, separate from Britain's rule.

The American Crisis was a collection of 13 papers written to encourage revolutionary soldiers during times when rations ran low and odds looked impossible.

The Rights of Man was written in response to an Edmund Burke piece that condemned the French Revolution. *The Rights of Man* not only spoke in favor of the revolution in France, but in opposition to monarchies in general. This writing prompted the British government to indict Paine on treason.

The Age of Reason was written by Thomas Paine as a statement of his religious beliefs.

________________ 1. "These are the times that try men's souls."

________________ 2. "The harder the conflict, the more glorious the triumph."

________________ 3. "The birthday of a new world is at hand . . ."

________________ 4. "The farce of monarchy and aristocracy, in all countries, is following that of chivalry, and Mr. Burke is dressing for the funeral."

________________ 5. "I believe in one God, and no more; and I hope for happiness beyond this life."

________________ 6. "When it shall be said in any country in the world, my poor are happy . . . the aged are not in want . . . the taxes are not oppressive . . . then may that country boast of its constitution and government."

________________ 7. "[The argument in favor of separating from England is based on] nothing more than simple facts, plain arguments, and common sense."

________________ 8. "What we obtain too cheap, we esteem lightly."

________________ 9. "To talk of friendship with those in whom our reason forbids us to have faith . . . is madness and folly."

________________ 10. "Heaven knows how to put a proper price upon its goods; and it would be strange indeed, if so celestial an article as freedom should not be highly rated."

________________ 11. "I consider myself in the hands of the Creator, and that he will dispose of me after this life consistently with his justice and goodness."

________________ 12. "To do good is my religion."

Name ______________________

Fightin' Words

Thomas Paine must have known that his words would sometimes stir up controversy. Historians contend that he probably knew that speaking on behalf of the life of the king to the French Assembly would likely mean his own death. Mr. Paine himself stated that he waited to write his views on religion until later in life as they might not be widely accepted. Still, when Thomas Paine felt his words were necessary for the progress of justice and freedom in the world, he did not stop himself from speaking. Answer the following questions below about your own ability to speak your mind.

1. When is it appropriate to speak your mind even if your words are not likely to be popular with the crowd? ______________________

   ____

   ____

2. Is it ever appropriate to keep thoughts to yourself even though you know them to be true? ______________________

   ____

   ____

3. Tell about a time you stood up for something even though you knew speaking out in favor of it would make you unpopular with your friends. ______________________

   ____

   ____

4. Thomas Paine made many enemies, but there are those who greatly appreciated his brave determination to speak in favor of what he believed to be right. On your own paper, incorporate some of the quotations below into a letter of apology to Thomas Paine for the ill-treatment he received from Americans at the end of his life.

   Ben Franklin on Thomas Paine: "I value myself on the share I had in procuring for America the acquisition of so useful and valuable a citizen."

   John Adams: "History will ascribe the American Revolution to Thomas Paine."

   French Ambassador (and later President) James Monroe in a letter to Thomas Paine in prison: "You are considered [by Americans] as not only having rendered important service in our own revolution, but as being, on a more extended scale, the friend of human rights, and able advocate of public liberty . . . To liberate you will be the object of my endeavors, as soon as possible."

   Thomas Edison: "I have always regarded Thomas Paine as one of the greatest of all Americans. Never have we had a sounder intelligence in this republic."

   Abraham Lincoln: "I never tire of reading Paine."

   Robert G. Ingersoll: "With his name left out, the history of liberty cannot be written."

Honest Abe

Background

Rags-to-riches stories about the life of Abraham Lincoln abound in literature and classroom textbooks. Most children realize that the legendary president was born into a hardworking farm family of modest means. They know that Lincoln's great mind was self-developed by fervent reading and that he attended less than a year's worth of formal schooling during his entire lifetime. Students may even be aware that Mr. Lincoln accepted defeat in many election campaigns and that he was not a very popular figure once he finally made it to Washington, D.C., as a U.S. Congressman representing Illinois in 1846.

Most students, however, are not aware of the string of odd jobs Abraham Lincoln held before he even entered law or politics. They do not know that his father and some of his friends thought the 19-year-old Lincoln to be a lazy boy. They are unaware that Lincoln as a young man co-owned a general store that declined quickly into bankruptcy. They are not privy to the fact that, while employed as a postmaster, Lincoln claimed the worst efficiency record in his region. They likely do not realize that even in his greatest hours of personal and political triumph, Lincoln was frequently subjected to devastating bouts of depression.

Abraham Lincoln himself embraced his failures and shortcomings. He once admitted, "I am not an accomplished lawyer. I find quite as much material for a lecture in those points wherein I have failed, as in those wherein I have been moderately successful."

Such failures notwithstanding, Lincoln also experienced much greater than "moderate success" by relying on diligence and honesty. "The leading rule for the lawyer," he said, "as for the man in every other calling, is diligence. Leaving nothing for tomorrow which can be done today." Additionally, he proclaimed, "Resolve to be honest at all events."

In this lesson students acknowledge the early "failures" in the life of the man who grew into the Great Emancipator and the glue that held our nation together in its most wrenching time of trial.

Teaching Activities

Lincoln Family Photos: Students create a photo album of Lincoln's family members as they learn about the lives of each.
Storyteller: Abraham Lincoln was such an avid jester and storyteller that historians still argue over the amount of truth in some of the tales he told. In this lesson students try to unravel Lincoln yarns.

Extensions

1. Numerous biographies have been written about Abraham Lincoln. Require each of your students to write a review of a different Lincoln biography. Students may choose from complete books or single chapters that have been included in books about heroes in general.
2. Require students to recite parts of famous Lincoln speeches.
3. Assign the study of specific Lincoln-related information such as his early life, his role in the Civil War, his foreign policies, or personal tragedies.
4. Write and illustrate children's books about Lincoln to be shared with younger students.
5. Act out circuit court procedures, Lincoln taking the oath of office, the Civil War, or other scenes from Lincoln's life.

Student Reading

Honest Abe

The contributions of Abraham Lincoln to the preservation of this nation and the abolition of slavery within its borders are well-documented. Indeed, stories of the courageous leadership of our sixteenth president have made Lincoln a national treasure and a worldwide legend. Stories of Mr. Lincoln's failures and shortcomings are less frequently told, but they too contributed to the strong and honest character of the remarkable man.

Abraham Lincoln was the first to admit shortcomings, failures, and rough beginnings. He freely shared stories of his challenging childhood in the midwestern wilderness where his family suffered through failed crops, hunger, land disputes, harsh winters, illness, and death. In a land and time that required a young boy to learn to use an axe as soon as he could lift it, Abraham Lincoln admitted he received less than a year's worth of formal education. He had to teach himself to read in the home of his two hardworking, but completely illiterate, parents.

As a young man, Lincoln worked jobs expected of a boy who had not completed much schooling. He farmed, and he operated ferries and flatboats on the Ohio River. Eventually, Denton Offutt hired Lincoln as a clerk in his New Salem general store where he became well-known for his storytelling skills, his intelligence, and his honesty. However, the small business soon after declared bankruptcy, and the unemployed Lincoln needed some place to turn. He turned to politics.

Abraham Lincoln ran for a seat in the Illinois House of Representatives and lost. So he went back into the grocery business. This time he and a partner purchased their own store. It fared no better than Offutt's business, and in a few months' time it had failed completely.

Next, Lincoln was appointed postmaster of New Salem, but he held the worst efficiency record in the region in that position. He would charge poor customers less for postage than was required or walk two miles to deliver a letter to a shut-in while leaving the post office door open, trusting his customers would pay for their stamps and pick up only their own mail. All the while, Lincoln also settled land disputes in the capacity of deputy surveyor of Sangamon County, drew and attested mortgages and filed legal papers for illiterates, completed poll books during local elections, and engaged in numerous forms of physical labor including rail splitting and mill work in an effort to earn money to pay off his failed business debts.

Then in 1834 Lincoln ran again for an Illinois House seat. This time he won. He won again in 1836, 1838, and 1848. Additionally, he obtained a law license in 1836 and rode the court circuit for three months each spring and fall, covering 8,000 square miles and serving 15 Illinois counties. Lincoln was on a roll.

Then he ran for a seat in the United States House of Representatives. He won, but his unpopular stance against President Polk's actions in the Mexican War made Lincoln's Washington, D.C., career so unsuccessful that he decided to return to law where he was competent and highly respected. Had not the Kansas-Nebraska Act passed in 1854, stirring up such ire in him, Lincoln later attested, he would never have reentered politics. And we would never have known the jack-of-all-trades who became the most legendary of presidents.

Name ______________________

Lincoln Family Photos

Learn about members of Abraham Lincoln's family as you read the paragraphs below. Then cut along the dotted lines and use each paragraph as a caption to be used in a Lincoln family photo album which you create using poster board or construction paper. Portray each family member in your album using sketches of your own or copies of photographs available in books about Lincoln or on the Internet.

Thomas Lincoln was Abraham's father. He was a hardworking farmer and skilled carpenter with a reputation of paying off his debts. Tom valued physical labor over intellectual pursuits and thought Abraham's interest in books to be idle laziness. Shortly after his son set out on his own, Tom is said to have complained to a neighbor, "I s'pose Abe is still fooling hisself with education. I tried to stop it, but he has got that fool idea in his head, and it can't be got out."

Nancy Hanks Lincoln was Abraham's mother. Like Thomas, Nancy was illiterate. She gave birth to three children: Sarah, Abraham, and another son who died in infancy. In 1818 Nancy died after drinking poisoned milk from a cow that had eaten wild snakeroot plants.

Sarah Bush Johnson was Abraham's stepmother. Thomas married Sarah, a widow with three children, about a year after Nancy died. Sarah was a fair and loving mother to Tom's children. She was perhaps the only influential adult in Abe's life who encouraged his learning. Abraham later referred to Sarah as "my angel mother."

Mary Todd Lincoln was Abraham's wife. She was one of seven children born into a wealthy Lexington, Kentucky, family. Mary was an excellent student and an ambitious and socially gifted adult. She also had the reputation of being a very loving parent. Many tragedies in later years, including the death of her husband and three of her four children, led to mental instability in Mary when she was old.

Robert Todd Lincoln was the first of four sons born to Abraham and Mary. Born in 1843 and dying in 1928, Robert was his parents' only child to survive into adulthood. His adult occupations included captain in the army, civilian lawyer, secretary of war under President Garfield, U.S. minister to England under President Harrison, and president of the Pullman Company. In 1875 Robert became estranged from his mother after contributing to her commitment to a sanitarium in concern of her mental health. However, there is some evidence that suggests they reconciled their relationship prior to Mary's death.

Edward Baker Lincoln was the second son born to Abraham and Mary. Little Eddie was a kind and gentle boy whose death, after an extended respiratory illness when the child was just under four years of age, pained his parents for the remainder of their years.

William Wallace Lincoln was born on December 21, 1850, the third son of Mary Todd and Abraham. Willie was an eager student who spent his free time writing poetry and doing math. For just over a year, he and his younger brother loved their home at the White House where they built a fort on the roof for use in playing "war games" and enjoyed the company of numerous pets who lived both in and outside their home. Willie was also a good companion to his parents whom he accompanied on trips of business and pleasure. At the young age of 11, Willie became ill and died. He was buried in Georgetown, but his casket was exhumed and boarded onto his father's funeral train three years later to be buried in Springfield with his father.

Thomas Lincoln was the youngest child of Mary and Abraham. He was an energetic child who loved to play pranks around the White House and cared none for scholarly studies. He locked doors, interrupted meetings, and rang call bells at random. "Tad," as he was nicknamed in keeping with his large head that made him appear to be a tadpole when he was an infant, loved both watching and performing in theater shows. After his father was shot, Tad made a concerted effort to mature. He attended school and accompanied his mother on travels throughout Europe. At the age of 18, he was overtaken by a cold that developed into a fatal lung infection that claimed his life. His mother was overcome with grief at the death of yet another of her children.

Name ______________________________

Storyteller

Although Abraham Lincoln periodically suffered the symptoms of depression, during the times he was not down, he was the life of a party. That is because he loved to tell a story. Later, the president became such a legend that people loved to tell stories about him. Read the following stories about Lincoln either told by himself or by others and decide which you think to be true based on what you know about the character of the man. Write FACT or FICTION in the blank provided to indicate your guess.

__________ STORY ONE: Biographers suggest that Lincoln first gained his title of "Honest Abe" while working at Denton Offutt's store where he was said to have walked six miles just to return change to a customer who had overpaid for her goods.

__________ STORY TWO: Lincoln is said to have gained respect from the "bad guys" and "good guys" in New Salem, Illinois, when he defeated the local "rough guy" in a wrestling match.

__________ STORY THREE: In a letter to an acquaintance, Lincoln wrote that he had promised a friend that he would marry her sister sight unseen. When Mr. Lincoln met the sister at last, he discovered she was large and unattractive, but she had a good mind and a kind personality. Although not attracted to the woman, Lincoln was determined to keep his promise; however, he did put off the wedding plans for as long as possible. At last, he conjured up the courage to ask for the woman's hand in marriage. It came as a great shock, then, when the young lady refused his offer. Mr. Lincoln was off the hook, he explained in the letter to his friend, but his ego did sustain an injury.

__________ STORY FOUR: As part of a political campaign, stories were told of Lincoln splitting wood for railroad tracks.

__________ STORY FIVE: One biographer wrote that a warrant for Abraham Lincoln's arrest was once served on the young man for operating a ferry service without a license.

__________ STORY SIX: One story suggests that as a young man, Abraham Lincoln saved the life of an older gentleman who had gotten drunk and fallen face down in a slushy puddle of freezing mud. As evening approached and temperatures began to drop, Lincoln lifted the man out of the puddle and carried him to a warm inn, saving him from freezing to death.

__________ STORY SEVEN: A neighbor of Lincoln when he was a young man told an interviewer that the boy liked to tell jokes and stories all the time.

__________ STORY EIGHT: Many biographers' stories suggest that Lincoln studied law on his own, often while seated outside under a shady tree or atop an old tree stump.

__________ STORY NINE: Many sources suggest that Lincoln used not only his remarkable knowledge of the law, but also an incredible ability to tell an emotional story to win court cases.

Sister Strike

Background

Coal is a natural resource found in abundance in the Appalachian region and interior basins of North America. It is valuable, not only in its natural state, but also when processed in various ways. Liquidated coal is used as a fuel in more than half of the nation's electric power plants. Distilled coal yields several useful chemical compounds to science and commerce including benzene and phenanthrene. Coal tar pitch, the residue left after distillation, is used in the production of steel, coke, and carbon electrodes used in batteries and roofing material.

Although available in a quantity not likely to become depleted for several centuries, coal is not simple to obtain. Surface and underground mining are complicated processes that utilize both sophisticated machinery and sheer brute force. Underground mining is the most hazardous occupation in the United States. Coal dust and methane gas combine inside underground mines and produce explosions without warning. Mining "rooms and pillars" cave in unexpectedly. Coal dust accumulates inside the lungs of miners causing black lung disease.

As challenging as the life of a coal miner is today, it was even more so at the turn of the century. In addition to the dangerous and dirty nature of his job, which he performed for 12 to 14 hours six days a week, a miner was also subjected to after-hours abuse prior to the acceptance and legalization of labor unions. Mining districts in the late 1800s were developed on private property located in the middle of nowhere. Coal company capitalists owned the homes their employees lived in and charged the miners high rents for the privilege of living in the shoddily built shacks. Company owners owned and operated the only store in the district, too, so they were not afraid to overcharge their customers. Miners might become angry enough to want to take their business to some far-off town away from the district, but they could not because they were paid in scrip that was accepted only at businesses within the mining district. Even mining town doctors, pastors, and teachers were commissioned by the company owners and paid for with a high tax placed on the miners.

When the United Mine Workers union challenged unfair mining district policies in the late 1800s and early 1900s, they were met with strong opposition from company owners. Striking miners were fired from their positions. Union-active miners were threatened, beaten, and sometimes killed. Company thugs and anti-union policies convinced many miners to steer clear of the union, but they did not convince Mary Harris Jones of anything.

In this lesson students read about a fearless old widow who helped organize miners and others in their efforts to establish unions and effect legislation in favor of fair business practices and safe working conditions.

Teaching Activities

Jones' Work in West Virginia: Students learn about Jones' efforts in West Virginia.
Creating Coal: Students learn about the processes involved in coal production.

Extensions

1. Visit a coal mine or invite a miner to display miner's clothing and instruments in your classroom.
2. Assign reports on the history of labor unions in other trades or in other nations.

Sister Strike

Mary Harris Jones was 81 years old when she read a newspaper article about striking coal miners in West Virginia. She had never been inside a mine shaft. She had no friends or relatives who labored as coal miners. The old dressmaker, who frequently donned a shawl and bonnet, seemed a highly unlikely candidate for the position of motivator for the Paint Creek Coal Company strikers.

The Paint Creek strikers of 1912 were not the first discontented laborers to welcome Mother Jones into their ranks. Mary had understood the plight of unjustly treated industrial workers since childhood. Her father was one of the thousands of Irish immigrants who gained employment constructing railroad tracks in America during the early 1800s. The very long hours, hazardous work conditions, and small paychecks Mr. Harris suffered were common complaints among blue-collar workers before legal regulations governed their treatment.

Still young Mary may never have fought for workers' rights had tragedy not struck in 1867. Before that year, Mrs. Jones' husband addressed such concerns. As a staunch member of the iron molders' union, George E. Jones fought for fair and safe working conditions for himself and his co-laborers. Mrs. Jones occupied herself raising the couple's four children.

Then yellow fever arrived in Memphis where the Joneses lived. Wealthy residents fled the city. Working-class families, financially unable to escape, watched their loved ones die. Mary's husband and all four of her children fell victim to the fatal epidemic. At age 37 Mary Harris Jones found herself alone in the world.

To support herself, Mary moved to Chicago and opened a dressmaking shop. Four years later, tragedy struck again. The Great Chicago Fire claimed Mary's business, home, and possessions. A lesser woman may have been defeated. Mrs. Jones was not. She looked beyond her own misery to the needs of others. From 1871 until the day her life ended in 1930, "Mother" Jones committed herself to what was once her husband's cause, a nationwide labor movement. She toured the country organizing unions, encouraging strikers, and supporting legislation in favor of workers' rights.

In 1912 Mother Jones offered her energy and determination to the struggles of Paint Creek strikers in West Virginia. Due largely to her efforts in Paint Creek and area mining districts, laws were passed to protect miners' rights and permit them to join unions. A little old lady who owned no more than she could fit into a small knapsack gave a great deal to the American worker of the past and present.

Name ______________________________

Jones' Work in West Virginia

Read about the following incidents in the adventures of Mother Jones as she encouraged coal-mining strikers in West Virginia in an effort to influence regulations in favor of fair and decent working conditions and pay. Then relate the stories to incidents in your own life by answering the opinion questions following each story.

1. Mother Jones was encouraging striking Southern Pacific Railroad machinists in California when she read about the Paint Creek miners' strike. Canceling a speaking tour, she hitched a train bound for West Virginia. Strikers in Paint Creek had been evicted from their company-owned homes and prohibited from traveling on their community's company-owned roads. Walking on railroad tracks and dry creek beds, the men led their families into surrounding hills where they pitched tents and chased off company guards who beat them up and tore down their shelters. Seeing Mother Jones renewed the spirits of the abused miners. They continued their strike while Mother made her way to a neighboring community that was facing challenges of its own.
   Tell about a time in your own life when you changed major plans because someone needed your assistance. ______________________________

   ____

   Tell about a time when you have lived in (or briefly experienced) less-than-ideal conditions such as the strikers did when they resided in tents. ______________________________

   ____

2. Cabin Creek miners, whom Mother Jones visited in West Virginia, were not members of the United Mine Workers union. Labor organizers who attempted to unite the men mysteriously disappeared or were chased out of town. Since the Cabin Creek Mining District was located on private property, company guards arrested any agitators who entered town on charges of trespassing. Mother Jones arranged a meeting outside town and persuaded many miners to privately join the union. The men were all fired from their jobs the next day when a company spy reported them as union members.
   Tell about a time when the assistance you provided someone did not turn out the way you had hoped. ______________________________

   ____

3. One day strikers in one West Virginia community walked along a public railroad track because they were prohibited from using the town's company-owned roads. When a couple company guards fired a machine gun in the direction of the migrating miners, Mother Jones approached the guards with no fear. She put her hand over the muzzle of the gun until her miner friends were safely out of its range.
   Tell about a time in your life when you have done something very brave. ______________________________

   ____

4. To reach striking miners, 80-year-old Mother Jones once waded through ice-cold creek water when not permitted to travel on company-owned roads.
   Tell about a time you have made a sacrifice for a friend. ______________________________

   ____

Name ______________________________

Creating Coal

Use an encyclopedia or reference book to help you determine which of the following statements about the production of coal are true. Indicate your response with a T or an F in each space provided.

______ 1. Although classified as a rock, coal is derived from vegetable material.

______ 2. Heat and pressure help to dehydrate peat deposits, transforming them into coal.

______ 3. Most coal which is mined today was formed hundreds of years ago.

______ 4. Russia and other former countries of the USSR produce the most coal in the world because they have the highest percentage of recoverable coal reserves in the world.

______ 5. Lignite, a classification of coal in which original plant remains can still be seen, is sometimes called *light brown* in reference to its color.

______ 6. Most often coal used in industry is ranked as bituminous coal, which is denser than lignite, but less dense than the hardest of all coals, anthracite.

______ 7. Anthracite is used as a domestic fuel thanks to the clean-burning flame it produces.

______ 8. Miners must go deep underground to collect coal.

______ 9. Three main methods of accessing an underground mine include cutting an opening into an exposed seam of coal, creating a sloped opening to a coal seam through a strata of rock, and developing a mine shaft which reaches a coal seam through a vertical opening.

______ 10. In conventional mining, miners use a single machine to cut, drill, break up, and load coal into a shuttle car that is transported to the surface on a conveyor belt.

______ 11. Previously exposed coal can be mined using a method called *longwall mining* in which jacks provide roof support to miners who extract large blocks of coal at once.

______ 12. Surface mining, also known as *strip mining*, can take one of three forms: area mining, contour mining, or open-pit mining.

______ 13. Although technology has been developed which helps keep the concentrations of methane gas and coal dust at low enough levels to prevent many unpredictable explosions from taking place in mines, underground coal mining continues to be the most hazardous occupation in the United States.

______ 14. A Federal Mine Health and Safety Act was passed in 1915 as a direct result of the efforts of Mother Jones in West Virginia.

______ 15. Nearly all modern coal-burning plants use smokestack scrubbers to protect the atmosphere from the dangers of sulfur and nitrogen compounds.

______ 16. Even though the method creates a great deal of pollution, some factories use a relatively new method of burning coal mixed with limestone in suspension above an incandescent bed of sand and air because it is inexpensive.

______ 17. Liquefying coal into a gaseous state is useful in the production of certain chemicals and fertilizers.

______ 18. Coal was used to produce most fuel gas prior to the 1950s when oil began to be used for that purpose.

______ 19. Most coal today is mined from surface mines and is used to fuel electricity-generating plants.

______ 20. Coal tar pitch, which is "left over" when coal is distilled, is disposed of in garbage dumps since it has no practical uses.

The Nonviolent Gray Panthers

Background

Aging is a natural phenomenon that decreases the metabolic rate as well as the speed of reflexes and the ability to reproduce in living organisms. Additionally, it increases a body's susceptibility to disease and injury and results in the degeneration and death of cells in the nervous system and beyond. The functional definition of old age in human beings, however, is defined by societal stereotypes rather than biological occurrences.

In industrialized nations, "old people" are usually defined by a chronological age. In the United States, people over the age of 65 are commonly considered senior citizens because that is the age at which pensions can be collected and senior discounts claimed. In traditional, nonindustrialized nations, old age is usually defined by physiological and mental changes rather than by chronological age.

While traditional societies tend to revere aged individuals, industrialized nations often demean the elderly. Art, music, the media, and pop culture glorify youthfulness. Employers, insurance agencies, and educational institutions—perhaps unintentionally—discriminate against the elderly.

In this lesson students read about a woman who founded a movement in 1971 directed at discouraging ageism and promoting intergenerational respect and cooperation. Maggie Kuhn turned a personal misfortune into a societal blessing when she publicly expressed her anger at being forced to retire at the age of 65 simply because she had celebrated a birthday.

Teaching Activities

Gray Panther Chronology: Students complete a time line of Gray Panther accomplishments.
Growing Old: Students learn facts and statistics about aging.
Consultation of Old and Young: Students work in Gray Panther-like networks to effect change in their homes, schools, and neighborhoods.

Extensions

1. Adopt a retirement center or nursing home. Establish pen pals between your students and the center's residents, organize an end-of-the-year party at the center, and encourage students to entertain with song, dance, talents, activities, and/or games.
2. Allow students to interview senior citizens about historical events or personal memories.
3. Create a class collage of photographs honoring the elderly.
4. Research and report on the role and treatment of the elderly in different societies.
5. Assign an essay reflecting on the pros and cons of growing old.
6. Assign reports on various aspects of aging including health and societal concerns.
7. Assign speeches arguing that senior citizens are or are not discriminated against in the United States.
8. Create a senior citizen cookbook and cook a senior citizen meal for the grandparents of your students based on recipes the grandparents provide.

Student Reading

The Nonviolent Gray Panthers

In August 1970 Maggie Kuhn celebrated a birthday and mourned a job loss. After 25 years working with the United Presbyterian Church in New York City, Kuhn was forced into retirement because she had reached the arbitrary age of 65. Kuhn was disheartened. She had been a productive employee in the world of work since 1925 when she taught junior high school briefly before working with the YMCA for 11 years prior to joining the United Presbyterian Church staff. Meaningful employment had been an important part of Maggie Kuhn's entire adult life.

The first people Kuhn expressed her disappointment to were five friends who also were being forced into retirement by national religious and social work organizations in 1970. The friends, who gathered to discuss age discrimination in the United States, soon found themselves talking about a variety of social concerns facing the old and young. Gradually Kuhn and her friends became convinced that discussing social problems openly was the first step toward correcting them.

Next, Kuhn and her friends arranged to meet with a group of Philadelphia college students opposed to the Vietnam War. The gathering of college students and retirees called themselves the Consultation of Older and Younger Adults for Social Change. Following their first successful convening, they arranged to gather again and again to discuss their common values and concerns.

The Consultation of Older and Younger Adults for Social Change evolved into a powerful public advocacy group quickly. By 1971 the Consultation claimed over 100 members. The next year, it adopted a name attributed it by a New York talk show producer—the Gray Panthers. In 1972 a Maggie Kuhn speech addressed to the 181st General Assembly of the United Presbyterian Church prompted hundreds of calls to the Gray Panther office. The group was gaining numbers and power.

The Gray Panthers began to work with other organizations including Ralph Nader's public advocacy groups, the American Association of Retired Persons, United Nations organizations, and presidential task forces to effect change. Over the years they have helped ensure African American representation at White House conferences on aging. They have effected legislation banning arbitrary-age forced retirement. They have exposed nursing home abuses, supported health care reform, and worked for peace, housing, and job opportunities for both the young and the old around the globe.

At its peak, the Gray Panthers claimed 60,000 members. Today, even after its founder's death in 1995, the Gray Panthers continues to claim 50 local networks throughout the United States. The forced retirement of Maggie Kuhn resulted in the formation of a large and powerful public advocacy group that continues to strive to perfect living conditions for all.

Name ______________________________

Gray Panther Chronology

Cut along the dotted lines to utilize the following achievements in the creation of a Gray Panthers' time line. Glue the following events in chronological order on a large strip of butcher paper or poster board. Illustrate at least five of the events on your time line.

1970 Maggie Kuhn meets with five friends to discuss her disappointment at being forced to retire.

1971 Kuhn and her friends gather with Philadelphia college students to form the Consultation of Older and Younger Adults for Social Change.

1972 The Consultation officially changes its name to the Gray Panthers.

1973 The Gray Panthers first addresses health issues affecting the elderly. Their work in that area will ensure fair prices on hearing aids, produce consumer directories of health officials, and effect legislation pertaining to Medicare.

1975 A national media watch task force begins to report on age stereotyping and discrimination in the media.

1975 The National Citizens Coalition for Nursing Home Reform is founded by a member of the Gray Panthers, Elma Holder.

1985 The Gray Panthers opens their first office in Washington, D.C.

1987 The Gray Panthers achieves legislation against mandatory retirement.

1993 The Gray Panthers sponsors an international People's Summit for Peace and report their findings to the United Nations.

1995 The Gray Panthers' founder, Maggie Kuhn, dies in her sleep just before her ninetieth birthday.

1996 The Gray Panthers cohosts the Age and Youth in Action Summit in Washington, D.C.

2000 The Gray Panthers claims 50 local networks throughout the United States.

Name ______________________________

Growing Old

Locate information on aging on the Internet or in a reference book to help you determine which of the following statements are true. Indicate your responses with a T for true or an F for false.

______ 1. A dog reaches old age long before a mouse does.

______ 2. Oxygen intake in humans decreases with age.

______ 3. A recent American Association of Retired Persons survey indicated that 34.4% of grandparents questioned had seen at least one grandchild in the month prior to being interviewed.

______ 4. As a person ages, cells throughout the body in such diverse systems as the skin and the nervous system die and are never replaced.

______ 5. Older people are more susceptible to diabetes mellitus because insulin is produced in lower amounts in their bodies.

______ 6. The American Association of Retired Persons reports that grandparents want most to pass on to their grandchildren ambition or the drive to succeed.

______ 7. One theory on aging suggests that the human body breaks down over time due to "wear and tear" much as a machine does.

______ 8. Another theory suggests that a person's life span is genetically predetermined and not affected negatively or positively by "wear and tear" or activity.

______ 9. In 1999 there were 34.4 million people over the age of 65 living in the United States. Thanks to the aging of the baby boomers, that number is on the rise.

______ 10. Nearly 35% of all elderly people describe their health as poor as opposed to 2% of the general public.

______ 11. About 28% of elderly persons in the United States are living in nursing homes or other institutions.

______ 12. Many more senior citizens live with their children in Japan than do so in the United States.

______ 13. In-home service programs for the elderly including meals-on-wheels and hospice nursing care are usually covered by Medicare.

______ 14. Individuals who receive retirement funds from their former employers are not eligible for Social Security benefits.

Name ______________________________

Consultation of Old and Young

Working together with your teachers at school, parents at home, and adults in your community, how could you improve conditions in your world? Gather in groups of five or six people composed of children and adults to make a single positive change by answering the questions below and implementing the plan your group devises.

SCHOOL CONSULTATION: Groups might include students, teachers, aides, parents, administrators, bus drivers, janitors, cafeteria workers, and/or school board members.

1. As a group, think of one condition that could be improved in your school or classroom using a simple, realistic plan. Describe your condition in need of improvement here: ______________________________
____
2. List a change or changes that would improve the condition you cited: ___________
____
3. Devise a step-by-step plan to implement the changes you cited:
   1. ______________________________
   2. ______________________________
   3. ______________________________

HOME CONSULTATION: Groups might include parents, children and/or extended family members.

1. As a group, think of one condition that could be improved in your home using a simple, realistic plan. Describe your condition in need of improvement here:
____
____
2. List a change or changes that would improve the condition you cited: ___________
____
3. Devise a step-by-step plan to implement the changes you cited:
   1. ______________________________
   2. ______________________________
   3. ______________________________

COMMUNITY CONSULTATION: Groups might include adult and children neighbors. As a group, think of one condition that could be improved in the neighborhood using a simple, realistic plan.

1. Describe your condition in need of improvement here: ______________________________
____
2. List a change or changes that would improve the condition you cited: ___________
____
3. Devise a step-by-step plan to implement the changes you cited:
   1. ______________________________
   2. ______________________________
   3. ______________________________

Shining Light into the Night

Background

In January 1933 the Nazi regime came to power in Germany. Immediately, it activated a two-part plan: control the world and rid the planet of Jews. For five years the Nazis concentrated on eliminating the Jewish community from economic life in Germany. Jewish civil service employees were fired from their posts; Jewish professionals lost their Aryan clients. Jewish business owners were forced to liquidate their companies or sell them at below-market value prices to non-Jews. Jewish property owners were subjected to special taxes.

In November 1938 after a German diplomat in Paris was assassinated by a Jew, the situation escalated. Two hundred and sixty-seven German synagogues were burned to the ground, countless Jewish shop windows were smashed, and 20,000 Jews were arrested. Following the "Night of Broken Glass," hundreds of thousands of Jews and other Nazi-target groups including Gypsies, homosexuals, and Communists, fled the country. Hundreds of thousands of others were unable to escape.

In September 1939 the Nazis initiated the world-domination element of their plan. They first occupied Poland, and later the former USSR, Italy, France, Denmark, Hungary, Belgium, Holland, and Romania. Jews in occupied countries received abhorrent treatment. In Poland they were raped, murdered, or forced to move into fenced-off ghettos where sanitation was poor, housing overcrowded, and the death rate high. In the former USSR, four special "strike squads" gunned down thousands of Jews on sight.

By September 1941 Jews from Germany and all German-occupied countries were being deported to ghettos and then to death camps throughout Poland and Germany. In the concentration camps, men, women, and children died of starvation, illness, shootings, and cyanide and carbon monoxide poisoning in gas chambers. By the end of World War II, nearly 6 million innocent civilian Jews, Slavs, Gypsies, and others were dead.

While thinking about the details of the Holocaust is uncomfortable at best for nations who did not act quickly to stop the atrocities, reliving the horror in memory must be much more difficult for Holocaust survivors. In this lesson students read about a man who insists on reliving the pain so that citizens of the world will remember the Holocaust for the sake of never permitting a similar tragedy.

Teaching Activities

Initiating Dialogue: Students consider safeguards for ensuring another Holocaust never happens in the world.
And the World Remained Silent: Students study the sequence of events that led to the United States' involvement in World War II.

Extensions

1. Research and report on the involvement of individual countries in World War II.
2. Research and report on the living conditions in ghettos and concentration camps.
3. Read and discuss with your class Elie Wiesel's classic *Night.*
4. With your class, learn more about the Holocaust. Visit the Museum of Tolerance in Los Angeles or the United States Holocaust Memorial Museum in Washington, D.C., or send away for information on either to share with your students.
5. Collect, display, report, and discuss current news stories that tell of war crimes that continue in the world today.

Student Reading

Shining Light into the Night

For a 16-year-old boy on the verge of manhood, suffering 12 months in Nazi concentration camps was not a great introduction to adult living. In fact, the magnitude of the atrocities endured by Elie Wiesel make it impossible to even imagine what the young man might have done with his adult life had it not been turned upside down before it had even begun. The lifelong impression left by the horrors he witnessed and experienced at 16 make it equally impossible to imagine Mr. Wiesel choosing any career other than the one he has.

Elie Wiesel is an authority on the Holocaust: a witness to the pain and death suffered by its millions of victims. Although excruciatingly aware that the atrocities of that event cannot be reduced to words or pictures, Wiesel keeps the memory of Holocaust victims alive through stories, pictures, and discussions designed to honor those who suffered and prevent future suffering.

In 1944, when Elie Wiesel was 16, he left his residence in what is now Romania along with his three siblings and two parents. The Wiesel family did not leave its hometown voluntarily. Sighet was a center of Hebrew learning where the Wiesels and their community's other 15,000 Jews could immerse their youth in the studies of Yiddish, Hebrew, and Bible history. Elie and his siblings enjoyed a happy, well-rounded childhood in Sighet.

Then the Nazis arrived. All of the Jews in Sighet were rounded up like cattle and deported out of town. Elie and his family were transported by train to the Auschwitz concentration camp in Poland. Almost immediately upon their arrival, Elie's mother and younger sister were gassed to death in a chamber where thousands of other human beings faced the same fate. Elie and his father were then separated from Elie's two older sisters. It would not be until after World War II ended that Elie would find that his sisters had survived the incomprehensible suffering.

For the next nine months, Elie and his father, too, suffered unspeakable torture and unthinkable living conditions that left both men sick, skinny, and demoralized. Then in January of 1945, approaching Soviet troops persuaded Nazi officials to march Auschwitz inmates to another camp in Buchenwald, Germany. Elie's father, weakened by dysentery, died of starvation en route. The much younger Elie made it to Buchenwald where he endured another three months of suffering before being liberated along with his fellow inmates by the United States Third Army.

The mix of anger, hatred, sorrow, survivor's guilt, and a myriad of other emotions resulting from his intense concentration camp experience left Wiesel in a state that could take a lifetime to sort out. Upon release from Buchenwald, the young man imposed a ten-year vow of silence on himself to allow himself time to accomplish at least the first step of the healing process.

For a full decade following 1945, he did not speak or write about anything that he had witnessed or experienced during the war. Instead, Wiesel studied literature, psychology, and philosophy in France and accepted a job in journalism, first writing for a Franco-Jewish newspaper, and later for a newspaper in Tel Aviv. Finally in 1956, encouraged by the French novelist François Mauriac, Elie Wiesel publicly told his story.

His first book, *And the World Remained Silent*—an 800-page semi-autobiographical account of the horrors Wiesel experienced, written in Yiddish—was soon abridged and translated into French and English. *Night,* as the book was titled in English, became a worldwide best-seller. Although hesitant to do so because of a continuous fear that words might trivialize the experience, Wiesel felt morally compelled to continue to write and speak out against racism and genocide and in favor of tolerance and an understanding and acceptance of Jews.

To date Elie Wiesel has written 36 works dealing with the Holocaust, Jewish education and acceptance, humankind's obligation to protest hateful acts, and the philosophy that life experiences can be understood through questions, not answers. He has lectured extensively on the Holocaust and issues surrounding tolerance. He has organized, led, and participated in numerous international conferences and panel discussions promoting peace and understanding across regional, ethnic, and race barriers. He served under President Carter on a presidential commission to establish the United States Holocaust Memorial Museum, and accepted from President Reagan the Congressional Gold Medal of Achievement. In 1986 Elie Wiesel was awarded the Nobel Peace Prize for his efforts to improve the living conditions of Jews worldwide and promote an international understanding of Jews as a people. Although no one would wish upon Elie Wiesel—nor any human being—the suffering he has endured, we thank him for the soul-wrenching decision he made to keep his horrible memories alive for the sake of both honoring the dead and preventing future genocide.

Name ______________________________

Initiating Dialogue

Elie Wiesel maintains mixed feelings about discussing the Holocaust. Although he believes it is important to tell, hear, and discuss the story for the sake of preventing future atrocities, he sometimes fears reducing the experience to words dishonors the memory of Holocaust victims. Still his conviction to prevent future tragedies by speaking out helps him overcome his fears. Wiesel has written over 30 books, helped develop the Holocaust Memorial Museum in Washington, D.C., and facilitated numerous panel discussions on the prevention of war crimes, the promotion of peace, and the lessons to be learned from a study of the Holocaust.

In honor of Mr. Wiesel's brave efforts to advance tolerance and peace, give serious consideration to the following questions which may be answered individually or in groups of two to four students.

1. Why might Elie Wiesel fear that discussing the Holocaust could dishonor its victims? Why does he believe it is important to discuss it anyway? ______________________________

   ____

   ____

2. What is a healthy response to demoralizing abuse? Retaliation? Forgiveness? Denial? Anger? Self-pity? ______________________________

   ____

   ____

3. Disrespect for human life, hatred, racial and ethnic prejudice, and ill-treatment of prisoners of war continue worldwide today. How can concerned citizens of the earth promote tolerance and peace around the globe? How can you promote peace within your classroom, community, and home? ______________________________

   ____

   ____

4. Why is it difficult and uncomfortable even for those who did not directly experience the horrors of the Holocaust to think and talk about it? ______________________________

   ____

   ____

5. Why do you think those under Hitler followed his command to torture and kill innocent people? Why do you think the world looked on in silence for as long as it did? How can we ensure that such abhorrent behavior is not repeated? ______________

   ____

   ____

Name ____________________

And the World Remained Silent

Read below about the sequence of events that occurred before the United States entered World War II and then answer the questions that follow.

January 1933	Hitler comes to power in Germany. Jewish citizens are subjected to discriminatory laws and taxes for the next several years.
March 1938	Germany annexes Austria.
November 1938	Following the assassination of a German diplomat in Paris by a Jew, synagogues in Germany are set on fire, Jewish store windows are smashed, and thousands of Jews are arrested in a night remembered as the "Night of Broken Glass."
March 1939	Germany occupies Czechoslovakia.
August 1939	Germany signs a nonaggression pact with the former USSR.
September 1939	Germany and the former USSR invade Poland. Jewish Poles are moved into fenced-off ghettos. The former USSR moves on to invade Finland and the Baltic States. France and Britain declare war on Germany.
April 1940	Germany invades France and the Low Countries. Jews living in occupied countries are deported to ghettos and concentration camps in Germany and Poland in growing numbers. Their bank accounts and belongings are confiscated by the Nazis.
Autumn 1940	Germany attacks Great Britain with night bombings and U-boat attacks.
June 1941	Germany suddenly invades the former USSR.
September 1941	Hermann Göring sends a directive to the chief of the Reich Security Office demanding the organization of a "final solution to the Jewish question." Jews in Germany are forced to wear yellow star badges. Tens of thousands of German Jews are deported to ghettos in Poland.
December 1941	Japan bombs Pearl Harbor. The United States enters World War II.

1. Why might the United States have waited as long as it did to enter World War II?

____

____

2. At what point during the above sequence of events would you have recommended that the United States enter the war? Why? ____________________

____

____

3. What events in the sequence above foreshadowed the establishment of concentration camps? ____________________

____

Miss Elizabeth Blackwell, M.D.

Background

The history of women in medicine is somewhat obscure. A third-century A.D. story written by a Latin author named Hyginus relates the account of a successful female physician who gained medical training by disguising herself as a man. In response to her phenomenal professional success, Athenian laws banning females from practicing medicine were said to have been lifted. Although the historical accuracy of the Hyginus story has been disputed, it is widely accepted that untrained women played a significant role in midwifery prior to the fifth century A.D., when educated male physicians began to take over their obstetric duties.

In more recent times, women were relegated to the sidelines of medicine, where they were expected to serve as nurses and assistants. In colonial America, for example, women were thought too modest and prudish to work in surgery or any aspect of medicine that exposed body parts. Colonial women were expected to cover most of their own skin in public and to refrain from any physical activity that might draw attention to their bodies. If they showed an interest in the health of other bodies beyond an empathetic desire to comfort a person in pain, females in early America were considered uncouth.

Elizabeth Blackwell knew the mind-set of her contemporaries had changed very little since those colonial days when she applied to American medical schools in the mid-1800s. Perhaps that is why she had the persistence to try 17 institutions before being accepted into New York's Geneva Medical College.

Since Dr. Blackwell's day, women physicians have become widely accepted and highly respected. In 1991 women comprised 36% of all medical school students in the United States. Over 20 percent of the professors at those schools were women. Nearly 20 percent of all medical doctors in the nation that year were female.

In this lesson students read about the challenges that faced the woman who paved the way for female doctors today—this nation's first female to earn a medical degree.

Teaching Activities

Doctor Blackwell's Day: Students put the medical practice of Dr. Blackwell into perspective as they research the state of medicine in the 1800s.
Women at Work: Students study statistics of women working in male-dominated fields today.

Extensions

1. Assign reports and/or time lines on the history of medicine from ancient times to the present.
2. Research the life of Emily Blackwell, Elizabeth's sister, who followed her into the medical profession.
3. Visit a hospital or invite guest speakers from the medical field to impress upon your students the multitude of diverse jobs available in medicine today.
4. Assign reports on "female firsts" in other fields including the first women in politics, the first women in aerospace, and the first women in business.
5. Assign reports on specific health issues including various diseases, diagnostic tools, medicines, and nutritional and health issues.

Miss Elizabeth Blackwell, M.D.

Elizabeth Blackwell was the first daughter—and the third child—born to a Bristol, England, couple who produced nine children. Samuel and Hannah Blackwell were intelligent, open-minded parents who insisted slavery was wrong, all people were created equal, and boys and girls should receive identical educations. Their liberal belief system shielded the senior Blackwells from social success, but it instilled in their children a determination to accomplish their goals regardless of obstacles or contemporary prejudices. In an age when most women were not employed outside the home and most men married women who supported their husband's interests rather than pursuing interests of their own, five Blackwell daughters grew up to have careers, and one Blackwell son married a women's rights activist who kept her own last name.

Elizabeth Blackwell grew up to become the first female medical doctor in America. More than once, she must have questioned her decision in the face of the nearly unilateral opposition she encountered, but she persevered.

Miss Blackwell set out on her path toward a medical career in 1847. Fifteen years earlier, at the age of 11, she had moved with her family to the United States after a fire destroyed her father's sugar refinery in England. Samuel Blackwell experienced little success in America, where his abolitionist views made him unpopular with other sugar producers who relied on the skills of slave labor. By the time Mr. Blackwell died in 1837, his family was nearly destitute. Elizabeth and her mother and two of her sisters opened a school to support their family. Elizabeth felt unfulfilled in her teaching position. She wanted to practice medicine.

Miss Blackwell applied to 17 medical schools before being admitted to Geneva Medical College in 1847. Administrators at institutions throughout the United States told Elizabeth she was not suited for the work of a doctor. Females were delicate and modest. They had no place in a career that focused on ailments of the vulgar human body. Even Geneva accepted Miss Blackwell's application on a fluke. The college dean, who did not want to take full responsibility for denying Elizabeth's application, put the matter to a vote of the student body. The all-male student body of the medical institution was convinced the whole matter was a hoax concocted by a rival school. In response to what they believed to be a joke, the young men voted to admit a woman to their campus. Geneva's dean abided by their vote.

Miss Blackwell's initial reception into Geneva Medical College was not a warm one, but she gained the respect of her school's students and faculty members by 1849 when she graduated at the top of her class. Upon graduation, Elizabeth Blackwell traveled to Europe to complete an internship. While there, she encountered misfortune. The young intern contracted ophthalmia while cleaning the infected eye of a patient. The infection left Blackwell blind in one eye and incapable of specializing in surgery as was her dream.

Dr. Blackwell returned to New York in 1851 ready to practice medicine in the capacity of general practitioner, but New York was not ready for her. Landlords were not willing to rent office space to a female doctor. Hospitals and clinics were not interested in hiring a female doctor. Patients were not anxious to call on a female doctor. So, Dr. Blackwell filled her time preparing a lecture series on the importance of good hygiene and physical education for women. Much to her surprise, the church basement, which she rented as a lecture hall, was filled to capacity on the evenings of her presentations. Dr. Blackwell's lectures won the respect and support of the Society of Friends, a Quaker organization.

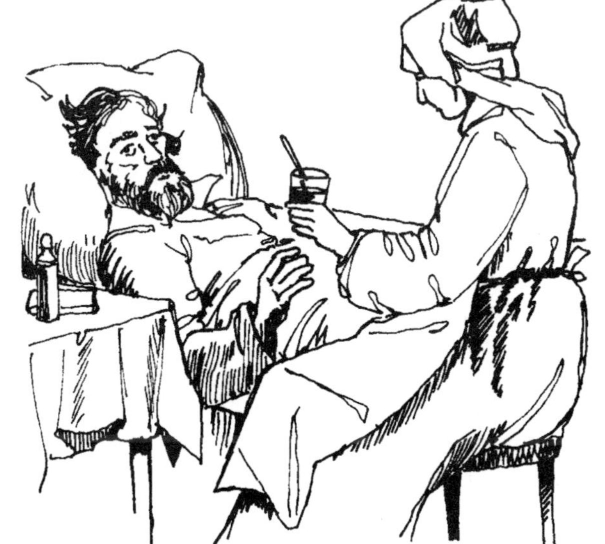

The Society of Friends helped Dr. Blackwell locate office space. Quakers called on Dr. Blackwell and encouraged their neighbors to do the same. Elizabeth Blackwell's business grew. In time, she was able to open a hospital for the poor called the New York Infirmary for Women and Children. Later she was able to raise the funds to add on the Women's Medical College of the New York Infirmary.

Several years later Dr. Blackwell returned to England and became the first female physician ever placed on the Medical Register of the United Kingdom. In 1871 she helped establish England's National Health Society. In 1875 she accepted a position teaching gynecology at the London School of Medicine.

Such great successes notwithstanding, Dr. Blackwell's professional life was never an easy one. Newspaper articles and strangers' comments suggested that she was vulgar and uncouth for choosing the medical profession. Hate mail criticized and threatened Dr. Blackwell's practice. When a patient with appendicitis died in Dr. Blackwell's office, it took the words of a coroner, who indicated the patient had no chance of survival, to calm an angry mob that had gathered on Dr. Blackwell's lawn to condemn the female doctor as a murderer. Through it all Dr. Elizabeth Blackwell, daughter of the enlightened Samuel and Hannah Blackwell, stood her ground. Female physicians today can thank her for doing so. In 1849 only one woman in the entire nation received a medical degree. Today about 36% of all U.S. medical students are women. In a myriad of medical specialty areas, women physicians are employed, accepted, and respected.

Name ______________________________

Doctor Blackwell's Day

Choose one of the following medical events or conditions listed below to research and report about to your classmates so that everyone can get an idea of the state of medicine during the era in which Dr. Blackwell practiced.

1. Nineteenth-century advancements in diagnostic procedures and instrumentation including the 1819 invention of the stethoscope and the 1896 accidental discovery of X rays led to the first-time identification of several diseases that are readily diagnosed today. Write one to two paragraphs on each of the following diseases first identified in the nineteenth century: Hodgkin's disease, Addison's disease, Parkinson's disease. Report your findings.

2. The nineteenth century gave rise to the first medical scientists to systematically study healthy and diseased human tissue under a microscope. Write a brief definitive description of histology. Report your findings.

3. Plant-breeding experiments conducted by Gregor Mendel from 1856 through 1863 stimulated the study of human genetics for the first time. Write a brief summary of the history of genetics. Report your findings.

4. Several discoveries during the nineteenth century led to the development of germ theory. Obstetrician Ignaz Philipp Semmelweis showed that unwashed hands transmitted infections to maternity patients. Joseph Lister proved bacteria were airborne. Write one paragraph about the discoveries that developed the germ theory, one paragraph defining the germ theory, and one paragraph describing the results of the development of the germ theory including the introduction of antiseptics to surgical work. Report your findings.

5. Anesthetics were first employed in the nineteenth century. Research and write about the conditions of surgery prior to the use of anesthetics. Report your findings.

6. The mosquito was first implicated in the transmission of malaria and yellow fever. Write one or two paragraphs describing each of the diseases. Report your findings.

7. The mid-nineteenth-century work of Matthias Jakob Schleiden and Theodor Schwann first proved that all plants and animals are made up of cells, and that cell division develops tissues and organs. Write a brief summary of cell division. Report your findings.

Name ______________________________

Women at Work

Statistics can often prove either side of an argument depending on how they are presented and interpreted. Use the following statistics reported in the mid-1990s and/or other contemporary statistics you locate on the Internet or in the news media to write a one-page persuasive essay. In your essay convince readers that women either have or have not made significant advancements in the world of work since the era of Elizabeth Blackwell.

Sixteen percent of scientists in the world today are women.

Six percent of engineers in the world today are women.

Women comprise 49% of all professionals.

Women comprise just over half the population, about 45% of employed workers in the United States, and about 30% of employed computer scientists.

Women comprise 7.8% of the professors in computer science and engineering schools. Eighty-four percent of Fortune 500 companies have at least one woman on their boards of directors.

Thirty-three percent of the middle and high school students enrolled in computer classes are girls.

Twenty-five percent of the people working in the field of law are women.

About 7,600,000 men are employed in construction in the United States while 784,000 women are employed in the same field.

Eighty-four percent of the medical doctors in the United States are men. Ninety-seven percent of nurses in the nation are women.

Thirty-six percent of the students enrolled in medical schools in the United States are women.

Fifty-five percent of working women provide half or more of their households' total income.

Seventy-one percent of single mothers are employed outside of the home.

Seven percent of all families in the nation are comprised of a stay-at-home mother, a working father, and one or more natural children.

Women constituted 6.5% of the faculty in computer science and computer engineering departments.

Mr. Chocolate Kiss

Background

The Industrial Revolution spurred on by James Watts' improvements on the steam engine design in 1769, the Edmund Cartwright invention of the power loom in 1785, and the Eli Whitney invention of the cotton gin in 1793 significantly changed the way people lived in Europe and America. By the beginning of the nineteenth century, many workers were employed in factories instead of fields. Consumers were buying products produced by machines rather than by hand. Residents were crowding ever-emerging cities where factories and retail outlets were located instead of living on extended family farmlands.

Benefits of the new age were impressive. Products that previously took weeks or months to produce by hand now flowed effortlessly from power-driven machinery. Inventors were inspired by the day's new technology to create unique time- and energy-saving devices. A powerful middle class grew out of the economic conditions brought on by the changes in technology and world trade.

Still the Industrial Revolution experienced a downside. Factory work was hot, dirty, difficult, and dangerous. Men and women put in 12- to 15-hour work days. Children worked nearly as many hours alongside the adults. By the middle of the nineteenth century, trade unions had emerged and laws had been passed to curb the problems that accompanied the revolution.

By the time Milton Hershey entered the manufacturing world in the late 1800s, a reasonable balance between the benefits and drawbacks of an industry-based economy had been reached. Factory owners and corporate giants worked with union leaders to provide employees with reasonable working conditions. Business owners banded together to form pleasant downtown regions in the large cities that had burst into existence overnight. "Company towns," complete with schools, post offices, banks, and row houses, were financed by a region's manufacturers to meet the basic social needs of a factory's employees and their families.

So Milton Hershey must have known that if he were to build a chocolate-manufacturing factory in the middle of nowhere, he would be expected to provide homes and essential businesses to its expected 600 workers. In this lesson students read how the die-hard candy manufacturer, who finally succeeded after six false starts, did provide his workers with a company town and more.

Teaching Activities

The Mennonite Way: Students learn how Milton Hershey's upbringing in the Mennonite faith might have influenced his desire to work hard and share his financial rewards.
The Town That Milt Built: Students learn about the town Milton Hershey inspired.

Extensions

1. Assign research and reports on other wealthy men and women who have given back to their communities.
2. Locate and download photos of Hershey, Pennsylvania, from the Internet.
3. Research the history of chocolate products in South America, Europe, and the United States.
4. Assign research and reports on the history of other famous brands of candy bars.
5. Write the Hershey Corporation for recipes or tourist information.

Student Reading

Mr. Chocolate Kiss

Henry and Fannie Hershey must have worried about the future of their young son, Milton. In addition to being the couple's only surviving child, the boy was a Pennsylvania Dutch-speaking, Swiss-German Mennonite in an English-speaking Protestant Christian world. As a result of the family's frequent moves around the state of Pennsylvania, Milton's education was limited to the completion of the fourth grade.

Milton Hershey's first ventures into business seemed to confirm his parents' probable fears. While still a teenager, Hershey was fired from his first apprenticeship with the editor of a Lancaster, Pennsylvania, German newspaper when he dropped his hat onto the printing press. In 1876 when he sunk a great deal of his uncle's money into a candy store in Philadelphia, he struck out again. Hershey thought his confections would tempt the throngs of people who drifted into the city that year in celebration of the 100th anniversary of the Declaration of Independence. In reality, the sweets he cooked up with the help of his aunt and mother did not even earn him enough money to pay off his uncle and his suppliers.

Milton Hershey did not give up. Somewhere between the newspaper job and the Philadelphia candy business, Hershey had successfully apprenticed with Joe Royer, a candy and ice-cream maker. With that success, young Hershey felt destined to manufacture candy himself. He moved from Philadelphia to Denver, where he established another candy store. It failed. He moved on to New York and established another candy store. It failed. He continued on to Chicago, where he established yet another candy store. It failed, too. Next, he established a candy store in New Orleans. It failed.

By 1886 when the 29-year-old Milton Hershey returned to Lancaster, Pennsylvania, his hardworking well-established Mennonite friends and family members shunned him as a drifting ne'er-do-well. He trudged on undaunted. A former employee of his 1876 Philadelphia store lent Hershey the money to send for his possessions in New Orleans and to set up shop in Lancaster. With the help of his mother and aunt once again, he began to manufacture and sell caramels. His "Hershey's Crystal A" recipe earned him substantial success at last!

When an English candy importer ordered a large supply of Hershey's caramels, the cashier at a Lancaster bank personally backed a loan to allow Hershey to produce the candy necessary to fill the order. In a short time, he had earned enough money not only to repay his loan, but also to build himself a fine home, and to finance several extended trips to foreign lands.

While visiting the World's Columbian Exposition in Chicago in 1893, Hershey became fascinated with a display of German chocolate-making machinery. He ordered the equipment and had it delivered to Lancaster, where he created the Hershey Chocolate

Company to manufacture a chocolate coating for his caramels. When the chocolate-covered caramels proved more popular than any other variety, Hershey sold his entire caramel plant for $1 million so he could concentrate on the creation of chocolate products only. Through persistent experimentation, he discovered a recipe for quality milk chocolate—a rare chocolate type in his day, usually imported from Switzerland. His secret-recipe milk chocolate made him a multimillionaire.

Initially, Hershey's chocolate company featured 114 varieties of chocolate, but eventually he narrowed its production line down to chocolate bars, chocolate coatings, a few novelty items, and cocoa products. The decision was a good one. By 1903 the Hershey Chocolate Company was so successful it needed to expand.

Hershey considered several locations for his new factory including Lancaster, Baltimore, New Jersey, and New York. Ultimately, he decided upon his birthplace of Derry Township, Pennsylvania. He built his huge factory, which would employ 600 workers, in the middle of farm country. By doing so, he knew milk would be readily available to him. Unfortunately, housing would not be available to his employees.

Hershey set out to alleviate that problem. He designed and built a model community to meet not only the residential, but also the social and cultural needs of his employees. Hershey's city plan featured homes, tree-lined streets, a school, a bank, a hotel, churches, and a grand park complete with a lake, picnic tables, wooded groves, and a bandstand and pavilion where vaudeville acts and theater productions took place frequently. By the tenth anniversary of the establishment of Hershey, Pennsylvania, he had added to his community a swimming pool, a golf course, a zoo, and a train and trolley system that made it convenient for tourists to visit Hershey and for employees of the factory to reside outside of town.

Then the Great Depression struck. The Hershey Chocolate Company could not employ all 600 of its workers. Other businesses in the community laid off laborers, too. So, Hershey organized the "Great Building Campaign." He employed out-of-work men in the building of a grand hotel, a complete community center, a senior hall, a modern office building, and a sports arena and stadium. During the Depression years, the town of Hershey boasted that no man was without employment. Following the Depression years, the town of Hershey boasted an even more fantastic community than before.

Milton Hershey made no great speeches, gave no substantial interviews, and wrote no exciting biography, but his deeds defined his character. The establishment of Hershey, Pennsylvania, and the "Great Building Campaign" were only two of numerous ways that Milton Hershey used his wealth to assist others and better the world. Mr. Hershey opened a boys' school designed to feed, clothe, educate, and care for orphaned boys. He financially backed a museum of Indian artifacts. In addition to cultural and recreational sites including golf courses, bowling alleys, an amusement park, and amphitheaters, he established a junior college, a library, and a hospital for the residents of his community. He supported his town's literary club, YMCA, and volunteer fire department. He organized a Hershey band and provided uniforms and equipment to Hershey sports teams. Milton Hershey's Mennonite upbringing taught him to work hard, produce a quality product, and use the money he earned to better the world. He did just that.

Name ______________________________

The Mennonite Way

Read the following information on Mennonite traditions and then indicate how Milton Hershey's faith might have influenced his life decisions.

The Mennonite faith is named for a man named Menno Simons who preached adult baptism and pacifism in the Netherlands during the 1500s. Because his followers refused to take an oath, assume state offices, or serve in the military, they were considered subversive and thus persecuted harshly. As a result, many of them fled their homes in the Netherlands and Switzerland for North and South America, Prussia, and Poland. Most of the "Old Order" Mennonites who moved to America settled in Pennsylvania.

Tenets of the Mennonite faith are recorded in the Dordrecht Confession. In general, the Mennonites are a community-based people who believe in living simple, honest, hardworking, and loving lives. Although they revere the Bible, they also believe God speaks directly to the hearts of individuals. Listening to one's own conscience, then, can direct one to proper decision making. Mennonites traditionally dress conservatively, reject worldly comforts, and use shunning as a form of punishment. The strict Amish Mennonites continue to farm and manufacture goods without the use of machinery, fasten clothes with hooks and eyes, worship in private homes, and speak Pennsylvania Dutch.

Traditionally, Mennonites have been a rural, set-apart people, although they have occasionally made political stands. The Mennonites were among the first to campaign for a separation between church and state as well as for the abolition of slavery. Mennonites do not support any wars and usually refuse to bear arms themselves.

Today the Mennonite Church in America claims about 109,000 members divided into two or three doctrinal sects, which are organized into regional assemblies and district conferences that support a cooperative effort to advance peace and end human suffering in the world at large. In addition to this work of the Mennonite Central Committee, the Mennonite Church financially supports schools of higher education and clergy who frequently work part time in the secular world.

1. In what ways was Milton Hershey's life influenced by his Mennonite background?

____

____

____

2. What things did Milton Hershey do in his life that did not reflect traditional Mennonite tenets?

____

____

____

Name ______________________________

The Town That Milt Built

Read about the stages in the development of two of the features of Hershey, Pennsylvania. Then illustrate the development of each place in pictorial time lines below.

MILTON S. HERSHEY SCHOOL

In 1909 Mr. and Mrs. Milton Hershey established a home and school for orphaned boys. The purpose of the school was to provide children with nutritious food, plain but adequate clothing, a clean and warm home, physical exercise, and a sound education to prepare them for useful trades. Initially, the school opened its doors to four boys. Three years after its establishment, when Mrs. Hershey died, Mr. Hershey endowed the school with his entire fortune. Over the years, the school has congratulated thousands of graduates thanks to Mr. Hershey's generosity. Today it nurtures and educates approximately 1,100 boys and girls.

HERSHEYPARK

Mr. Hershey provided for the cultural needs of his community from the beginning. His original town included a gorgeous wooded public park including a lake for boating and fishing, an outdoor bandstand, and an amphitheater that were completed in 1907. By 1909 the park had added a photography gallery, a scenic railroad, a running track, a tennis court, and a bowling alley. The next year the Hershey Conservatory and Greenhouse was opened. In 1911 a carousel and outdoor pool were added to the park. A grand ballroom graced the park in 1913, and a bigger stage was built in 1914 to accommodate the members of big bands who played at the park, including Glenn Miller and Louis Armstrong. A 6,000-seat convention hall was added to the park in 1915 as well as the Hersheypark Cafe. In 1916 the Hershey Zoo opened its doors. A number of amusement park rides were introduced to the park during the 1920s. A golf course was added in 1929. A 16,000-seat stadium was built in 1935. By 1945 approximately 25 amusement park rides graced the park including a huge carousel and the Wild Car roller coaster. Additional rides have been added each year since that time, and today Hersheypark is a grand place of recreation and fun.

Milton S. Hershey School Pictorial Time Line of Development

Hersheypark Pictorial Time Line

Banking That Builds

Background

Various forms of banking have been in existence since ancient times. Early Rome and Babylon both operated extensive state-managed systems. Religious military orders safeguarded valuables and granted loans in Medieval Europe. The Renaissance period gave rise to highly successful European banking families who lent money and financed international trade.

The modern bank system—based on the concept of liabilities exceeding and being more liquid than reserves—was born in England during the seventeenth century. English goldsmiths during that period safeguarded and temporarily lent out precious metals. The paper receipts, which the goldsmiths issued to depositors, gradually grew into acceptable currency throughout the nation. In little time, the banknotes in circulation exceeded the value of the gold being safeguarded. Although unsecured in a day before deposit insurance, the system resulted in economic expansion and provided a model for today's banking systems.

The first established bank in the United States was a private institution regulated and supported by the federal government. The 1791 Bank of the United States was an effective institution, but its charter was not renewed in 1811 due to questions about its constitutionality. The Second Bank of the United States opened in 1816 but soon suffered the same fate.

During the next three decades, "free banking" allowed numerous groups and individuals to open banks all over the United States, but most of these early institutions were unable to survive the economic strains of the Civil War. Besides, different banks offered different types of notes during that period, making currencies in the United States ineffective.

Gradually, state and federal regulations established a common currency and an insured system of depositing and loaning money. By the early 1900s, banks in the United States resembled those we are accustomed to doing business with today, with one exception. Turn-of-the-century banks did not serve the "little man." Short-term commercial loans to wealthy individuals or businesses were virtually the only loans in existence. Lower- and middle-class citizens were more inclined to deposit their money under a mattress than in a bank. Then on October 17, 1904, the Bank of Italy opened its doors, and the world of banking greeted the "little man."

In this lesson students read about the grade school dropout who founded what is now the second largest bank in the United States.

Teaching Activities

Earthquake! Students write newspaper accounts of San Francisco earthquake stories.
Banking on Your Arithmetic Skills: Students complete story problems related to banking.

Extensions

1. Design a student-operated bank in which students who spend time reading or completing extra assignments are awarded banknotes that can be redeemed for prizes.
2. Research and report on the advancements in technology used in banking over the years.
3. Have students study bank brochures that indicate the numerous functions of a bank today. Then allow them to create brochures for an imaginary bank of their own.

Student Reading

Banking That Builds

In 1901 a financially secure 31-year-old partner in a wholesale produce business sold his interest in the company to his employees and settled into early retirement. Amadeo Peter Giannini had left school at the age of 14 to assist his stepfather in selling fruits and vegetables. The boy's sincere and dedicated approach to business quickly earned him a fine reputation and a partnership position. By the age of 19, the young man was a full-fledged business co-owner. Now at 31, he was a wealthy married man ready to retire—which he did, temporarily.

Then in 1902 A. P. Giannini was invited to join the board of the Columbus Savings and Loan Society in San Francisco, California. Giannini accepted the offer, but the institution's other directors soon wished he had not. In an age when financial institutions catered to wealthy individuals and established industries, Giannini promoted a radical theory. He was convinced that lending money to working-class citizens would not only be profitable to lending institutions, but also advantageous to entire communities. Homes, businesses, and infrastructure could develop and give back to a town if someone would take the risk of lending to the "common man."

Columbus Savings and Loan would not take that risk. So, in 1904 A. P. Giannini left the institution and converted a saloon across the street from it into a bank of his own, retaining the business's bartender as an assistant teller. Through a door-to-door promotional campaign, Giannini built up a healthy clientele of working-class citizens who deposited and loaned money from his bank designed to build and support communities. Additionally, he lent money to not-yet-proven industries including the motion-picture and wine-making industries in California. Within two years' time, Giannini's Bank of Italy (later named the Bank of America) had become as successful as he and his stepfather's produce business had been years before.

Then on April 18, 1906, Giannini's converted saloon crumbled to the ground along with thousands of other businesses and homes that fell victim to the Great San Francisco Earthquake. Undaunted, Giannini borrowed a produce wagon and loaded its bed with gold, coins, and securities he was able to collect from the ruins of his bank. In the days and weeks following the earthquake, when other bankers insisted on remaining closed until able to inventory damages, Giannini set up shop on a North Beach dock. Improvising a desk from two barrels and a wooden plank and operating out of his produce wagon, Giannini offered quake-stricken individuals and small businesses rebuilding loans "on a face and a signature." Such honest business dealings and the pioneering of home loans, auto loans, installment credit, and branch banking helped Giannini build what was at the time of his death in 1945 the largest bank in the nation.

Name ______________________________

Earthquake!

While A. P. Giannini was busy searching for gold coins in the rubbish of his devastated bank following the 1906 San Francisco earthquake and fire, editors of the *Daily News* were struggling to write stories about the disaster. Like Giannini they had to improvise on their business practices a bit. When their building lost water and power, they moved their operations to a small shop on Mission Street and began providing San Francisco's residents with written reports of stories from the quake. Imagine you are a San Francisco newspaper reporter in 1906. On your own paper, write a newspaper story account of one of the following aspects of the disaster.

1. Every one of San Francisco's orphanages suffered damage in the 1906 earthquake. Only one infant died in the disaster, but many children were shaken from their beds, marched into open lots, and finally ferried into Marin County to safety. Children in orphanages watched walls crumble, windows crash, and doors fly off their hinges. In some cases, children panicked and were difficult to calm down. In other cases children were composed and helpful, assisting their wards in getting clothing and blankets out of unsafe buildings before abandoning them forever.

   Write a story about the experiences of children in the 1906 earthquake. Include comments about what might be in store for them now that their homes have been destroyed.

2. Many people wrote about the interesting behavior of animals during the earthquake and fires in San Francisco. Dogs seemed to sense disaster and ran in packs from areas where fires were burning to areas that were safe. Rats did the same. In fact, rats became such a problem in the temporary shelters following the quake, that the city government paid children and adults alike for each rat they killed.

   Write a story about the packs of rats and dogs in the city following the quake.

3. Hundreds of stories of heroism and the rebuilding of San Francisco following the 1906 earthquake suggest that the disaster brought people together and created a sense of family among survivors.

   Write an imaginary story of heroism in the setting of the 1906 earthquake or fires in San Francisco.

4. Many San Francisco citizens wrote personal accounts of the earthquake and fire in the months and years following the disaster. They wrote about being shaken from bed, water flinging from tubs, walls cracking, glassware and windows breaking. They wrote about men, women, and children pushing their belongings to safer areas in wheelbarrows as fires approached their homes. They talked about watching their homes being dynamited in an effort to stop the spread of the fire. They talked about building shelters out of sheets in the city's parks and waiting in long lines for soup and water. They talked about lost loved ones, fear, and sorrow.

   Write an imaginary personal account of the 1906 earthquake.

Name ____________________

Banking on Your Arithmetic Skills

Use logic and your arithmetic skills to help you solve these word problems related to banking.

SCENARIO ONE: Two months ago, you opened your first checking account with $500. You chose an account that charges you a monthly service fee of $5.50. In the first month, you wrote seven checks in the amount of $220 and deposited a $150 check. During the second month, you deposited a $250 check and wrote three checks in the amount of $154.00.

1. After your service fee was assessed, how much money did you have in your account at the end of the first month? ____________
2. After your service fee was assessed, how much money did you have in your account at the end of the second month? ____________
3. Disregarding the initial deposit necessary to open the account, in which month did you deposit more than you spent? ____________
4. Would you have more or less money in your checking account at the end of the two-month period described above if you had opted to pay $1.00 for each check you wrote instead of the $5.50 service fee you chose to pay? ____________

SCENARIO TWO: Your bank offers a savings account that pays 7.5% interest monthly for money placed in the account for one year or more, but penalizes you 3% for withdrawals made before the close of the year. It offers another savings account that pays only 3.5% monthly interest but allows you to withdraw money at any time.

1. You plan to place money in your savings account that you intend to use to buy a car in three years. Which savings account would be best for you and why? ____________

   ____

SCENARIO THREE: Figure the ending balance for the account described here:

BEGINNING BALANCE $2,340.00

CHECKS

# 123	$54.00
# 124	$1.28
# 125	$45.89
# 126	$567.00

ATM WITHDRAWALS

1/5	$20.00
1/8	$100.00

DEPOSITS

1/12	$232.00
1/15	$75.00
1/28	$341.00

SERVICE CHARGE

1/31	$4.50

INTEREST

1/31	$7.50

ENDING BALANCE: ____________

The Colonel of Chicken

Background

Business is a word that refers to commercial and industrial operations that govern the production, distribution, and sale of services and goods. The three major forms of business ownership are *individual proprietorships, partnerships,* and *corporations.* Mr. Harland Sanders was familiar with all three forms, but he became rich and famous only after embarking on a single business practice that incorporated aspects of each: *franchising.*

In franchising, business owners or corporations grant permission to other individuals or companies to sell their products, use their name, apply a method of production, and/or implement a comprehensive method of conducting business which they have invented or developed. Both sides of the franchise stand to win in the bargain. The person who sells franchising rights is able to spread his/her name or product far beyond his/her hometown factory, and the person who buys the franchising rights is able to benefit from the financial status and time-tested ideas of a company that is already successful.

The term *franchises* is rooted in the French word for "privilege." As early as the Middle Ages, kings granted franchises, or rights, to subjects who wished to hold fairs or hunt on royal land. By the mid-1800s the concept had evolved into its current usage. The Singer Sewing Machine Company began writing distribution franchise agreements in 1851. Municipalities began granting franchises to utility companies around that same date. By the mid-1900s, the end of World War II and the baby boomer-driven economy in the United States gave rise to countless franchise businesses including the famous McDonalds chain and Colonel Sanders' own Kentucky Fried Chicken restaurants.

However, when Harland Sanders began to share his famous fried chicken recipe with other entrepreneurs, he was not a typical young serviceman looking to start a new business following his return from war. Harland Sanders was a 65-year-old man whose restaurant had been squeezed out of business by an encroaching highway that drove customers right past his town of Corbin, Kentucky.

In this lesson students read how a 65-year-old man living off a monthly Social Security check in the amount of $105 worked his way into millions over the course of his remaining 25 years of life.

Teaching Activities

Business Alternatives: Students consider the pros and cons of various business arrangements.
Keeping Secrets: Students learn how the Colonel keeps his secret recipe secret.

Extensions

1. Allow students to create their own secret recipes by adding choice ingredients to a basic cake or cookie recipe. See if students can guess one another's added ingredients by tasting the finished product.
2. Require students to guess the 11 herbs and spices included in the Colonel's Original Recipe® chicken. How many herbs and spices overlap in the guesses of your students?
3. Assign reports on the business arrangements of local businesses. Which are run by individual proprietors, which by partnerships, and which by corporations? Which are franchises?
4. Locate products that are manufactured by individually or partner-owned factories and others that are made by corporate entities or conglomerates.

Student Reading

The Colonel of Chicken

In 1896 six-year-old Harland Sanders' father died. The boy's mother suddenly found herself in the business world, and Harland suddenly found himself in the kitchen. As eldest of three children, it was young Harland's job to mind his siblings and help with cooking chores. By the time he was seven years old, Harland was already accomplished at preparing Midwestern cuisine typical of his Indiana community.

Harland's first jobs outside the home, however, did not showcase his culinary talents. From about the time he was 10 until the time he was 15, the precocious child worked for earnings on local farms. At 15, he became employed driving a streetcar. At the young age of 16, he became a private in the United States armed forces stationed in Cuba.

Harland Sanders would not cook for a living for another 24 years. Even then, he only did so as a sideline to his business selling gas. From age 16 to age 24, Mr. Sanders was a busy man. At different times he served as a railroad fireman and a justice of the peace. He sold insurance and operated a steamboat ferry. Finally, at the age of 40, he settled into what looked to be his final career as the owner of a gas station.

Harland Sanders' Corbin, Kentucky, gas station was a popular stop for weary travelers—not only because he provided gas and automotive products at a reasonable rate, but also because he was known to serve a hungry passerby a fine meal on the dining room table in the living quarters of his service station. The food Mr. Sanders provided hungry travelers was so good, customers began visiting the service station for no other reason than to eat.

So, Harland Sanders changed occupations again. He purchased a motel and restaurant across the street from his gas station and began serving fine meals full time. The public was pleased. By the late 1930s Mr. Sanders' culinary skills had gained him the title of "Kentucky Colonel" from the state's governor, and his restaurant had earned a listing in a respected restaurant review book.

Then in the early 1950s, an interstate highway was built in Kentucky that routed travelers right past Corbin. The 65-year-old Colonel Sanders sold his restaurant and motel and collected Social Security payments of $105 a month while he formulated the plans for yet another business. Colonel Sanders was convinced that customers would enjoy the specially seasoned chicken he fried if only they could get at it. So, Colonel Sanders brought the chicken to the people. He traveled all over the United States with batches of his spice mix packaged in bags and boxes in his back seat. In each town, he offered to fry chicken for restaurant owners. As expected, the owners liked what they tasted. They ordered more spices from Harland who phoned them home to his wife. Claudia mixed the flour and spices according to her husband's specifications, packaged the secret recipe seasoning, and shipped the packages by train to fill her husband's orders.

By 1964 Kentucky Fried Chicken® restaurants around the country were so successful that the franchise was eagerly purchased by a group of investors. Colonel Sanders himself bought the first 100 shares of stock, but he did not really need the dividends. The six-year-old cook had finally grown into a million-dollar chef.

Name ____________________

Business Alternatives

Although corporations comprise most of the business arrangements in the United States today, there do exist partnerships and individual proprieties as well. Below are listed some advantages and disadvantages of each arrangement. Match the arrangements with the statements that describe their pros and cons.

Business Alternatives		
Sole Proprietorship	Partnership	Corporation

ADVANTAGES

____________ 1. This business arrangement allows a single owner to ensure that the quality of his/her service or product meets his/her expectations because he/she alone manages or personally assigns the management of all aspects of the business.

____________ 2. This business alternative is a separate legal entity chartered by the state and responsible for the liability of debts incurred by an unsuccessful venture.

____________ 3. Many of America's farmers have found this business alternative to their liking for hundreds of years. They can build their homes on their own property and manage their own affairs under this arrangement.

____________ 4. This business alternative, which has influenced the economy of industrialized countries more and more since the start of the Industrial Revolution, has encouraged great growth in product availability and technological advancements.

____________ 5. This business arrangement allows two or more individuals to pool their financial and creative resources together in the establishment of a new business.

DISADVANTAGES

____________ 1. Being an intangible entity, this business arrangement is always in need of regulation adjustments to ensure that results of its practices not become unfair. For example, many abuses in the trust system that grew out of this arrangement brought about the end of that system.

____________ 2. This business is an infrequent choice for new business owners in today's world because it requires a single person to possess enough capital to cover all start-up costs.

____________ 3. This arrangement puts both partners at financial risk by holding them equally responsible in case of incurred losses or debts.

____________ 4. This type of arrangement sometimes forces smaller companies to close their doors since the size of this type of operation allows for large stores to be filled with a wide selection of reasonably priced goods.

____________ 5. This alternative often takes the personal touch out of business interactions by relying heavily on computerized systems to answer questions, manage billing, and address customer concerns.

____________ 6. This business arrangement makes a business owner personally liable for all business debts.

Name ____________________

Keeping Secrets

In the 1930s, while operating his restaurant in Corbin, Kentucky, Harland Sanders mixed herbs, spices, and flour on a specially cleaned concrete slab on his back porch until he came up with a delicious recipe for fried chicken coating. After he sold his own restaurant and hit the road, Mr. Sanders kept his recipe a secret even while offering it to other cooks for use in their restaurants. If the owner of a restaurant liked the sample chicken Mr. Sanders fried up using the spice formula he carried in his car, the owner would order more of the coating mix. To meet the orders, Mr. or Mrs. Sanders would mix up batches of the spices using the formula which they had memorized. The recipe was not ever written down until Mr. Sanders became a very old man.

Today Colonel Sanders' Original Recipe® is locked in a safe in Louisville, Kentucky. Only a handful of people who have been sworn to confidentiality know what herbs and spices are listed on that locked-away recipe card. Even the employees who blend the spices for Original Recipe® coating mix do not know the entire recipe. One company blends part of the recipe into a mixture which it delivers to another company that adds the remainder of the necessary ingredients to complete the formula.

Why is all this secrecy necessary? In complete sentences answer the questions below about keeping secrets.

1. List at least two reasons keeping Colonel Sanders' Original Recipe® a secret is good business: ____________________

   ____

2. What makes "good" secrets, such as surprise parties and Christmas presents, such fun?

   ____

   ____

3. Do you think it is good for a government to keep certain information from getting into the hands of its own citizens? Why or why not?

   ____

   ____

4. How can keeping secrets sometimes hurt others? What type of secrets hurt people?

   ____

   ____

5. What types of information should never be kept secret?

   ____

   ____

6. If a friend of yours told you about a secret problem that you know an adult could help with, would you keep your friend's secret or tell an adult? Why?

   ____

   ____

The Supercomputer of a Superbrain

Background

The United States government maintains a list of the 20 most difficult puzzles confronting the nation's top scientists and engineers. The 20 Grand Challenges recently had to be revised in recognition of the solution to one of its problems: how to inexpensively simulate the flow of oil inside reserves.

Oil is located inside the pores of underground rocks. Frequently, oil companies have to pump gas or water into an oil field to coax the petroleum to flow to nearby wells. A well that sucks out oil too fast can go dry before all of an area's oil has been recovered, leaving available reserves trapped until another expensive well is drilled. Therefore, it behooves an oil company to conduct a computer simulation of the speed and direction of oil flowing within a given field before initiating drilling. However, until 1989, the only computers capable of performing the calculations required to simulate oil flow were $20 million supercomputers.

In 1989 a young college student working on his doctoral dissertation developed a new approach. Philip Emeagwali utilized the Internet to connect 65,536 personal-sized computers to a single Connection Machine. Together his system of computers successfully calculated oil flow not only at a fraction of the cost of supercomputers, but also at a speed that broke all calculation records in the computer world. As a result, oil companies are now able to track oil flow and recover a much greater percentage of petroleum from any given field.

In this lesson students read about the challenging beginnings of a child who grew up to write the fastest computer program in world history.

Teaching Activities

Mrs. Emeagwali: Students learn of the fascinating life of Philip Emeagwali's wife.
The Mind of a Scientist: Students discover the views of Philip Emeagwali and explore their own views in relation to them.
Role-Playing Greatness: Students act out the life of a scientist who experienced false starts.

Extensions

1. Expose your students to basic computer programming by utilizing one of the many instructional programs written for students at their grade level.
2. Assign reports on contemporaries who work to advance the field of computer science.
3. Demonstrate the speed of even the simplest calculating machine by pitting a student with a pencil and paper against a student with a calculator in a race to answer a list of mathematical computation questions. Alternatively, demonstrate the speed of working with computers in general by pitting two groups in your class against each other in an information scavenger hunt. Devise a list of trivia questions and allow one group to research their answers on the Internet and another group to locate them in reference books in the library.
4. Emeagwali's Connection Machine achieved the speed of 3.1 billion calculations per second. It was capable of completing its oil flow simulation that took into account the behavior of oil at 8 million individual points in one sixth of a second. As a means of putting that speed in perspective, allow students to use science texts and other references to create a list of other phenomena that occur in less than a second.

Student Reading

The Supercomputer of a Superbrain

In 1989 Philip Emeagwali became the first solo winner of the Gordon Bell Prize (considered the Nobel Prize of computing) for writing a computer program that could perform calculations at the speed of 3.1 billion per second. That was twice the speed achieved by the program written by the 1988 team of prize winners and 24 times the speed of the program written by the 1987 winners. Emeagwali's solo achievement would have been incredible even for a person raised in a world of technology, but Philip had never seen a computer until his first year of college!

Philip Emeagwali was born in Onitsha, Nigeria, in 1957. By the time he had reached the fourth grade, he was already considered his school district's mathematical genius. Marveling at his extraordinary ability to calculate sums and products, his teachers and classmates called Philip "Calculus." Some of his neighbors were actually convinced that the child used magic to solve problems of geometry and trigonometry at such an early age.

The officials at St. George's Grammar School in a nearby town thought Philip used other means of achieving mathematical success. When he scored 100% on a one-hour-long entrance exam which he completed in five minutes at the age of 10, the school's officials refused to accept the student on the grounds that he must have cheated on the test. Actually, he achieved his score honestly, but it did not matter. In a land where education is not provided by the government, Philip's father could no longer afford school fees. Besides, Nigeria was in the midst of a bloody civil war, and the Emeagwali family was forced to flee their homeland. For years, Philip, his parents, and his seven brothers and sisters lived in refugee camps and abandoned buildings eating only the meager food charity organizations were able to provide.

All the while, Mr. Emeagwali continued to stress the importance of education to his children. He personally instructed Philip in mathematics, until the boy surpassed his father's knowledge and skill. Then Philip studied on his own out of textbooks located in area libraries. By age 17 Philip Emeagwali had earned the equivalent of a high school diploma and a General Certificate of Education from the University of London by passing examinations. He had also won a scholarship to Oregon State University.

Philip Emeagwali's respect for education continued to grow in the United States. The young man was introduced to his first computer and his first college classroom. He fell in love with both of them. After earning a bachelor of arts degree in mathematics at Oregon State, Emeagwali continued his studies at George Washington University where he earned two master's degrees, one in ocean and marine engineering and one in civil and environmental engineering. Then he achieved a master's degree in applied mathematics at the University of Maryland. Finally, he was ready to work on a doctoral degree in scientific computing.

Emeagwali enrolled in the University of Michigan and began work on his dissertation. The goal of his research was to employ the use of thousands of computers connected by the Internet in calculating the flow of petroleum in oil reserves. If successful, his project could save oil companies millions of dollars by providing them with an inexpensive tool for completing a task only $20 million supercomputers were capable of doing in the absence of Emeagwali's plan. Philip Emeagwali liked to use a metaphor from agriculture to explain his project. While supercomputers represented a team of eight oxen that could pull a cart easily, Emeagwali was convinced that 65,536 chickens pulling in coordination might be able to accomplish the goal even more effectively.

Emeagwali was right. The 65,536 personal-computer-sized processors he had linked to his Connection Machine were able to simulate a few hours' worth of oil flow in a field in one sixth of a second. His "coordinated chickens" had together achieved the speed of 3.1 billion calculations per second. It was a speed that broke all records in the world of computer computations. It was a speed that earned Philip Emeagwali the Gordon Bell Prize in computer engineering.

By simulating oil flow inexpensively, Emeagwali had solved one of the most challenging puzzles facing scientists and engineers in the nation. And he did not stop there. Philip Emeagwali has worked as a civil engineer in constructing traffic highways and operating hydroelectric dams. He has put his programming skills to work for the United States National Weather Service and the United States Army High Performance Computing Research Center. He has earned world records for solving the largest partial differential equation with 8 million grid points and the largest weather forecasting equation with 128 million grid points. Inspired by complex patterns and behaviors in nature including the tessellated pattern of a honeycomb and the organized behavior of bees, Philip Emeagwali is currently working on another revolutionary computer called the hyperball. It will assist scientists in calculating the long-term effects of global warming and greenhouse gases.

The poor Nigerian refugee who had to drop out of school at 14 years old due to a lack of finances has earned numerous awards and distinctions in his work to help solve important problems in society. And somewhere along the way, Philip Emeagwali, the superbrain, created the fastest computer in the world.

Name ______________________________

Mrs. Emeagwali

Read about the accomplishments of Dale Emeagwali (Philip Emeagwali's wife) below and then write about the careers of other husband-and-wife teams who have achieved great success either together or separately in related or unrelated fields.

> Dale Emeagwali is a medical scientist who earned her Ph. D. from Georgetown University School of Medicine in 1981. She has completed research in microbiology, enzymology, virology, molecular biology, and biochemistry at several colleges and institutions throughout the United States including the National Institute of Health and the University of Michigan Medical Center. Additionally, she teaches undergraduate-level college courses and inspires an interest in science in children by conducting workshops for fourth- through twelfth-grade inner-city youth. She has earned numerous honors for her work including a listing in *Who's Who in the World, Who's Who in Technology, American Men and Women of Science,* and the *International Who's Who in Medicine.* Most recently she claimed the National Technical Association's 1996 Scientist of the Year Award in recognition of a discovery that furthers the understanding of cancers that develop in the blood system.

Use an encyclopedia to assist you in writing about the accomplishments of these other husband-and-wife pairings. (Note that some of these men and women worked in the same field, or even together, while some became successful in unrelated fields.)

1. Roald Dahl and Patricia O'Neal: ______________________________

2. Georgia O'Keeffe and Alfred Stieglitz: ______________________________

3. Pierre and Marie Curie: ______________________________

4. Elizabeth Barrett Browning and Robert Browning: ______________________________

5. Jane Fonda and Ted Turner: ______________________________

Name ______________________________

The Mind of a Scientist

Read some of the personal views of Philip Emeagwali below and then write in complete sentences why you agree or disagree with each.

1. Dr. Emeagwali suggests that reading stimulates creativity. As long as one is thinking critically as he reads, Philip believes all reading materials are valuable—from children's books to complex mathematical texts.
   Do you agree that all forms of reading stimulate creativity? ______________________

   ____

   ____

2. Dr. Emeagwali believes that the job of a scientist is to solve problems that confront society. He has utilized his engineering and programming skills to help forecast floods, help predict the spread of AIDS, and better understand the complex movement of oil in oil fields. Currently he is working on a computer called the *hyperball* that will help scientists determine the long-range effects of global warming. The supercomputers he programs significantly assist in solving problems in varied fields including health, energy, meteorology, and the environmental sciences. Do you agree that the job of a scientist is to solve problems that confront society? ______________________

   ____

   ____

3. Dr. Emeagwali is inspired by nature and other cultures in his work. Sometimes a human being can find the solution to a problem by studying how a plant or animal solves a similar problem. Sometimes a person of one culture can gain a completely new perspective on a puzzle confronting him/her when he/she looks to the approaches, values, and behaviors of another culture.
   Do you agree that studying nature and other cultures can help scientists solve problems? ______________________________________

   ____

   ____

4. As a successful scientist and a native of Nigeria, Dr. Emeagwali feels obligated to inspire Africans to work in the fields of science, technology, and invention so that they can improve their standard of living and overcome prejudices that stifle the amount of education, respect, and valuable jobs they receive.
   Do you agree that successful individuals are obligated to inspire others to succeed?

   ____

   ____

5. Dr. Emeagwali highly values education. He is convinced that the idea that one needs to be a genius to be a scientist is a myth. He believes individuals can be trained to be scientists.
   Do you agree that scientists can be trained? ______________________

   ____

   ____

Name ______________________________

Role-Playing Greatness

Philip Emeagwali lived through poverty, a lack of formal education, and a civil war. Read about four other scientists who experienced challenges in their lives. Then, in groups of two or three, choose one to research further. Based on your group's research, write a one-act play in which your group members act out a scene or several scenes from the life of the scientist you chose.

BUCKMINSTER FULLER has been dubbed the "Planet's Friendly Giant." In addition to introducing the world to the geodesic dome design used in Disneyland's Epcot Center, he also patented several other environmentally friendly inventions. In 1927 it would have been difficult to guess Mr. Fuller would have benefited humanity at all. Following the death of his first daughter, Mr. Fuller found himself jobless, broke, and frequently drunk. About four years into his mourning, Mr. Fuller had a revelation. He would stop drinking and start seeing how much difference one man could make in the world.

NIKOLA TESLA was fascinated with science and invention since he was a young boy. One of his first "inventions" was a motor powered by 16 june bugs glued to a spinning disk. Nikola went on to perfect the use of alternating current electricity. Tesla suffered through frequent illness, however, both in childhood and adulthood. Additionally, he was not a very good businessman. Because he did not patent all of his ideas or market himself and his skills successfully, the world remembers Thomas Edison, although Tesla completed a lot of the work.

JOHN BACKUS is the computer scientist who invented the first high-level computer language called FORTRAN. His contributions to computer science have been numerous, but Mr. Backus did not always think technology would be his field of study. In elementary and high school, he failed many subjects, primarily because he hated to study. Later, in college, he took medical courses thinking he might like to be a doctor. He hated medical school and dropped out. Backus did not know what he wanted to do next, but he did know what he wanted to own. He wanted to own a nice high-fidelity stereo, but nice ones did not exist in the late 1940s, so Backus enrolled in radio technicians' school so he could learn how to build one. His success at the school led to Backus's subsequent enrollment at Columbia University, and his eventual employment at IBM, where he introduced many significant advancements to the computer world.

JOHN FORBES NASH is a mathematical genius who has contributed important theories to mathematics and economics including his Nobel Prize-winning game theory. In addition to bursts of brilliance, however, Mr. Nash has also suffered mental breakdowns on several occasions during his lifetime. In an effort to lessen the stigma of mental illness, Mr. Nash speaks frankly about his periodic encounters with schizophrenia.

The Greatest Showman on Earth

Background

Today's technology offers entertainment seekers countless in-home options. Thanks to radios, televisions, telephones, VCRs, camcorders, and computers, we can listen to rock concerts, cheer on sports teams, view or film theatrical performances, wander through virtual fine art museums, converse with faraway friends, or play Internet Monopoly with strangers across the globe without ever leaving our living rooms.

During the mid-1800s, in-home entertainment options were significantly more limited. A family might play cards, read books, or sing songs to the accompaniment of a piano or guitar-playing relative, but little else was available to do indoors. The first record players would not become available to the public until 1877. Radios would not enter the scene for another 50 years beyond that. Television entertainment would wait even longer in the wings. So fun-seekers of the mid-nineteenth century often looked for amusement outside the boundaries of their homes.

The entertainment families found outside their homes often took the form of free community gatherings. "Work parties" including quilting bees and barn raisings joined neighbors in loosely structured events that involved both work and play. Saturday night dances and Sunday afternoon church picnics that relieved community members of the weariness brought on by their weekday chores were organized by volunteers. Seasonal events such as holiday parades and harvest parties featured the musical and comical talents and gardening and cooking skills of area residents. Although traveling plays and concerts periodically drew in a region's wealthier members, most entertainment forms of the day were not moneymakers but simple community-sponsored events that featured regional goods and talent.

Born into this era, P. T. Barnum recognized an undeveloped market when he saw one. Everyone loved a parade or harvest party. The hardworking citizens of our young, growing nation hungered to put down their plows and be entertained on occasion, and P. T. Barnum believed they would be willing to pay money should the fun offered be freakish and fantastic enough.

In this lesson students learn how the insistence of P. T. Barnum to put on the grandest show on earth enticed him to weather the good and bad results of the enormous financial risks that made up his rather entertaining life.

Teaching Activities

Barnum's Menagerie: Students learn about some of the more popular acts managed by Mr. Barnum.
Under the Big Top: Students learn the history of the circus.

Extensions

1. Organize a class circus in which students perform unusual or entertaining talents.
2. Require all students to dress in circus clothes or wear clown makeup on a day dedicated to the study of the history of the circus, mimes, clowns, and other live entertainment forms.
3. Assign a paper comparing and contrasting live entertainment with movies and/or music CDs.
4. Facilitate a debate on whether animals are mistreated when involved in circuses, zoos, or rodeos.

Student Reading

The Greatest Showman on Earth

The originator of "the Greatest Show on Earth" was not an instant success in the circus world. In fact, he did not even *officially* enter the circus business until after he had celebrated his sixtieth birthday. Prior to that time, he *did* display curiosities and incredible feats, but not as part of any organized circus—and not without his share of failures.

It all began when P. T. Barnum reached age 25. The young man had been employed since the time he was 16 when his father died and left his oldest son to provide for his mother and four younger siblings. In those early days, Barnum tried his hand at many trades. He peddled hats, he ran a boarding house, he worked in a general store, he sold lottery tickets, and he owned and edited a small newspaper. Phineas seemed unsuited to all he tried. In writing stories for his newspaper, for example, Mr. Barnum was so blunt and unkind that he once landed himself in jail for a six-month stay on a libel conviction based on his words against a local Calvinist minister. Upon his release, supporters of his views offered him a 40-horsemen, local band-supported welcome-back-to-freedom parade, and P. T. Barnum was never again the same. At once, the man recognized two things: the media is a powerful tool in the stirring up of emotions, and Phineas Barnum was in the wrong business.

Barnum liquidated his newspaper, quit his job selling lottery tickets and clerking at a general store, and sunk every dollar he had to his name into the purchase of an old slave named Joice Heth. For years, Joice Heth had traveled around the East Coast with previous "owners" who claimed she was the 161-year-old former nanny of George Washington. The stories she told about the father of our country were fascinating, but her show was not a big moneymaker, until Barnum came along. Mr. Barnum introduced Joice to countless New England small towns and big cities through exaggerated newspaper stories and fantastic posters and flyers before he even set out on tour. In town after town, he learned Joice Heth was a big hit before she even rolled across the city limits in her horse-drawn carriage proceeded by a regal brass band and parade. She provided Barnum, in fact, with over $1,500 dollars a week, until . . .

In 1836, six months after P. T. Barnum began touting the woman around New England, the 80-year-old Joice Heth died. That's right, an autopsy on the body of the alleged nanny to young George Washington proved a bit young herself to have performed the duties of nanny some 125 years earlier. P. T. Barnum suffered his first defeat. He was publicly exposed as not having displayed the former nanny of a national hero, but simply a popular hoax.

Still, hoaxes proved profitable and Barnum continued his use of entertaining tricks. He next purchased a slave who could juggle and sing. When a heckler from one town's crowd suggested he could perform more tricks than Barnum's juggler, Barnum used the man's claim to his benefit in towns to come. At every subsequent tour stop, Barnum hired a man to suggest he could do so when Barnum offered a money prize to anyone in the crowd who could keep up with his juggler. The competition between the professional juggler, who always eventually won, and the secretly hired man from the audience became a successful part of the act. So successful was his juggling show, in fact, that when his slave ran away at a stop in North Carolina, Barnum darkened his face and performed the act himself to avoid disappointing his audience. Soon, he purchased a paddleboat, hired other performers, and took his show up and down the Mississippi. That is when hardship number two struck. Great Depression sufferers did not have spare change to budget for entertainment, so they went without.

P. T. Barnum was undaunted. In 1841 he returned to New York and purchased Scudder's American Museum, a house of stuffed animals and natural artifacts. Mr. Barnum renamed the museum Barnum's American Museum and modified its displays. Alongside the animals and artifacts, he exhibited a singing dwarf, Siamese twins, a supposed petrified giant, a bearded lady, a tattooed man, and a "mermaid" fashioned out of a fish's tail and a monkey's head.

Thanks again to an unprecedented onslaught of exaggerated advertising, P. T. Barnum's strange exhibit center became one of New York's most patronized museums. It brought in $100,000 within its first three years in business. Charles Stratton, the museum's singing dwarf, renamed General Tom Thumb, became one of America's first superstars. He performed to the applause of citizens all over this nation and kings and queens throughout Europe.

Mr. P. T. Barnum built his family, which now consisted of a wife and two daughters, an enormous mansion in Connecticut. He very successfully promoted a Swedish opera singer on the first United States tour conducted by a foreign musical performer. He gave up drinking, wrote an autobiography, and helped finance the establishment of a new community called East Bridgeport.

Then tragedy struck again. When an East Bridgeport clock maker whom Barnum financed went bankrupt, he took Barnum with him. P. T. Barnum had to part with his museum. He also would have had to sell his home, except that it burned to the ground. The now penniless exhibitor began to exhibit himself. He wrote a book about how to make money, and he set out on a lecture tour wherein he shared the story of his life.

Thanks again to fantastic advertising, P. T. Barnum's exhibit was a success. His lectures raised the funds not only to pay off his debtors, but also to repurchase his museum, which became popular again until it was burned down during the Civil War. Although it was rebuilt after the fire, the museum burned to the ground yet another time. The 60-year-old Phineas Taylor Barnum decided then to retire. Until . . .

A friend suggested that Mr. Barnum take his performers on the road, or on the rails, rather. In 1871 Barnum agreed and *officially* entered the circus world. The Barnum circus soon merged with the Bailey circus. The "Greatest Show on Earth" employed a 65-freight-car, three-engine train; 500 men; and 200 horses. The circus brought in over one million dollars a year.

Mr. Barnum soaked up the success. He served a term as mayor of East Bridgeport. He was elected to the Connecticut General Assembly twice. At the time of his death at age 81 in 1891, Mr. Phineas Taylor Barnum, the man whose own life was a fascinating exhibition of gains and losses, could claim the position of "Father of Modern-Day Advertising and Fantastic and Freakish Performances" and inventor of the paying crowd.

Name ______________________________

Barnum's Menagerie

Read about the following Barnum circus acts. Then, in a one-page essay written on your own paper, compare and contrast the Barnum circus with modern forms of entertainment. What makes an event or act entertaining? Has our view of entertainment changed since the days of Barnum? In what ways has it stayed the same? Use comparisons with modern forms of entertainment to make your points.

Jumbo, the Elephant

In 1861 a scrawny baby elephant was captured in Central Africa by an employee of England's London Zoo, where he began a 20-year career of carrying thousands of children around the zoo grounds on his ever-growing back.

Then in 1882 P. T. Barnum offered the London Zoological Society $10,000 for the elephant. Fearing the aged beast may eventually become distempered, the society was happy to unload the creature. Queen Victoria and the English public were not so excited with the prospect of bidding adieu to their beloved national treasure, but Barnum would not relent to their cries of protest.

On Easter Sunday of 1882, Jumbo reached the shores of New York City where he was greeted by thousands. Over the course of the next three years, he became the main attraction of the "Greatest Show on Earth." Then on September 15, 1885, Jumbo was hit by a train while crossing a railroad track. The hide and skeleton of his 11.5-feet-tall, 6.5-ton, 24-year-old body were reconstructed and displayed originally with the circus and later in a museum where they remained on exhibit until destroyed in a 1975 fire.

Jenny Lind

In 1850 P. T. Barnum persuaded a famous Swedish singer to conduct a tour of the United States. Highly popular in Europe, the Royal Theater School-trained pianist and vocalist was a virtual unknown in the United States until Barnum began to bombard the press with stories of her life, tours, and talents. Dubbed in the stories "the Swedish Nightingale," Miss Lind was so popular with the American public by the time of her arrival in New York that her ship was greeted by nearly 40,000 fans.

Barnum continued to popularize Jenny once she began touring in the states by auctioning off tickets to her concerts for as much as $650 apiece. Many wealthy and famous Americans enjoyed Jenny Lind's performances along with throngs of others who pushed and shoved to purchase tickets to one of the 95 concerts she performed at the Castle Garden in New York or the other shows she presented in 19 other cities. Within one year's time, Barnum had grossed $712,000 from Jenny Lind concerts, and Jenny herself had earned $175,000.

Tom Thumb

Born Charles Sherwood Stratton, Tom Thumb was renamed by P. T. Barnum in honor of a tiny character from the Knights of the Round Table stories. Tom was a five-year-old, 25-inch tall, 15-pound dwarf when Barnum met him. After teaching him to sing, dance, act, mime, and tell jokes, Barnum exhibited his young friend first in his museum and later through tours around the United States and Europe. Tom became a huge success and worked for Barnum for years, entertaining crowds of "nobodies" as well as such notables as Queen Victoria, Prince Albert, and Abraham Lincoln.

The Cardiff Giant

On October 15, 1869, a man named George Hull instructed his cousin William Newell to hire workers to dig a well at a specific location on his property. Two years earlier, Hull and Newell had buried a slab of rock that Hull had carved to resemble a petrified giant at the very location in which the well was to be dug. The laborers dug up the "giant," and news of the discovery spread like wildfire. By the end of the day Mr. Newell was charging 25 cents to spectators who drove to his farm to see the hoax. After a month, he was charging 50 cents and offering round-trip stagecoach rides from regional cities to his farm. Soon, he and his cousin had made a killing off their fake giant by selling it to a banker named David Hannum, who believed it to be a true petrified man.

The carved rock slab, named the Cardiff Giant, gained the attention of P. T. Barnum when theories about its authenticity reached national newspapers. While some experts believed the rock to be the petrified body of an ancient giant, others thought it to be the remains of an old statue. Barnum thought it to be a moneymaker. He offered Hannum $50,000 for the creature, but was refused.

Undaunted, Barnum manufactured his own Cardiff Giant. He put his creature on display and made bold media claims that he had, indeed, purchased the true Cardiff Giant from Hannum, and that the giant Hannum now displayed was a fake.

Hannum took Barnum to court for calling him a liar, Hull admitted the original Cardiff Giant which he sold to Hannum was a hoax, and a judge ruled that Barnum could not be sued for calling Hannum's giant a fake since it was.

Chang and Eng

The original Siamese twins were born in 1811, connected by a tissue that stretched between their chests. The king of Siam condemned the boys to death upon hearing about their connection which he considered a bad omen. Luckily, Chang and Eng's mother did not obey the decree and kill her children, and the king did not press the issue.

By the time the boys were 14 years old, their father had died and their mother had agreed to an offer by a British merchant named Robert Hunter and his American partner Captain Able Coffin to exhibit her children for a fee. They performed under Hunter and Coffin until their twenty-first birthday and then went into business for themselves. Audiences were fascinated with their graceful coordination in running, somersaulting, back flipping, and playing sports. Doctors, who examined them in each toured city to prove their authenticity, were amazed by their ability to seemingly read minds and perceive sensations such as tickling when administered to the opposite twin.

By 1839 Chang and Eng had earned enough money to stop touring. They settled in Wilkesboro, North Carolina, where they managed a store, ran a 1,000-acre farm, and married two sisters and raised two families migrating between two separate homes. All told, Chang and Eng fathered 21 children.

Financial hardships forced the twins to return to the stage on more than one occasion, and at one time to be exhibited in Barnum's American Museum. Although they sometimes contemplated an attempted operation to separate themselves (especially after arguments that twice became violent), they did remain connected until their final night on January 16, 1874, when Eng died three hours after Chang's death at age 63.

Name ______________________________

Under the Big Top

Determine which of the following statements about the circus are true. Indicate your response by recording the word TRUE or FALSE in the blank provided.

________ 1. The term *circus* can be used to refer to a tent or building where a performance of exhibitions and animal shows takes place, the performance itself, or the troupe of performers who entertain.

________ 2. The first circuses featured juggling acts to which horsemanship, aerialist acts, and animal performances were later added.

________ 3. Circuses originated in Russia in the late 1700s.

________ 4. Many early nineteenth-century European circuses were traveling shows that featured a few acrobats, a rope dancer, and a juggler.

________ 5. P. T. Barnum was the first American to organize a circus in this country in 1870.

________ 6. Most early circus performances were free of charge.

________ 7. The last modern circus act to be introduced was the flying trapeze performance that made its debut in 1859.

________ 8. P. T. Barnum was not the first individual to implement the use of multiple rings in circus shows.

________ 9. Upon the deaths of Barnum and Bailey, the Ringling Brothers took the lead in circus entertainment when they purchased six circus companies including Barnum and Bailey's operation.

________10. The Golden Age of the Circus is said to have ended when the Ringling Brothers announced in 1956 that the big top was dead. Mounting labor and freight costs ended the tent circus era and condemned most performances to the less romantic permanent building.

________11. The world's most popular circus today is a troupe based in Australia.

________12. James Anthony Bailey is considered by historians to have been the more intelligent, organized, and energetic member of the Barnum and Bailey team, although his shyness and disdain for public attention kept him from flaunting his brilliance.

Picture Perfect

Background

The landscape of New Mexico reflects millions of years of geographic evolution. Extensive mountain ranges throughout the state owe their existence to both ancient volcanic activity and the very gradual uplifting of massive chunks of the earth's surface above the lands surrounding them. Large basins between the ranges, filled with sand, gravel, and soil, stand as testimonials to the effects of long-term erosion. Plateau regions in western New Mexico chronicle time with their display of hundred-, thousand-, and million-year-old brightly colored rock layers comprising cliffs, mesas, buttes, and canyons.

Although considered by many desert country, New Mexico is actually home to all major biomes with the exception of tropical rain forests. At various locations and elevations, everything from alpine tundras to wooded forests can be found within New Mexico's borders. In areas where alpine glaciers receded slowly, pockets of "historical gardens" brag diverse plant life variations living side by side in single locales.

Animal life in New Mexico varies according to region. High elevation forests are home to black bears, mountain lions, deer, and bighorn sheep. Lower elevations in southern New Mexico claim smaller nocturnal animals including bats and kangaroo rats. Prairie dogs and coyotes roam the grasslands of the state's eastern border. A variety of lizards and snakes resides throughout the generally mild, sunny, and dry state.

Adding to the geographic intrigue of New Mexico are some unique circumstances. The state's location puts it in the pathway of both Pacific and polar continental air fronts providing for a wealth of weather and vegetation possibilities. Crossing the state from north to south is the Continental Divide, which is made up of ridges separating rivers that flow to the Pacific from rivers that flow to the Atlantic.

Sightseers and scientists alike have studied the land formations and biomes that comprise New Mexico, but only one woman can claim to be the state's artistic geographer. During her long lifetime, Georgia O'Keeffe painted landscapes as diverse as New York City and the backwoods of Texas, but her renditions of the beauty of New Mexico became her signature pieces. New Mexico was her home and her love. O'Keeffe's strikingly pure paintings of the dry animal skulls and desert flowers that grace New Mexico's landscape have made it the home and love of the world as well.

In this lesson students read about the lean years in the life of an artist who thought an illness might leave her unable to ever paint again.

Teaching Activities

Visualizing Beauty: Students illustrate descriptive scenic passages.
"Mr. O'Keeffe": Students learn about the contributions of Alfred Stieglitz to the development of photography as an art form and the American movement of modernism.

Extensions

1. Introduce your students to replicas of O'Keeffe artwork located in art books in your school's library.
2. Conduct an art activity in which students attempt to imitate the style of O'Keeffe.
3. Create a collage of magazine art featuring scenery of New Mexico and the rest of the nation.
4. Compare and contrast O'Keeffe's work with realist, surrealist, and abstract styles.

Picture Perfect

Georgia O'Keeffe was born an artist. Her earliest memory involved sensing the brightness of light all around her as an infant. By elementary school, the child had discovered that artistic endeavors allowed her to express her individuality more freely than any other subject. By the time she had reached her teen years, Georgia was determined to grow into a recognized painter.

Miss O'Keeffe set out to learn the necessary skills for her chosen profession. By her sixteenth birthday she had already completed five years of private art lessons. Upon her graduation from high school in 1905, she attended first the Art Institute of Chicago and then New York City's Art Student League.

Then Georgia O'Keeffe's dream began to fade. A male classmate, referring to the conventions of the day that did not celebrate female artists, told Miss O'Keeffe she would never become a recognized painter. When her father's business ventures failed, O'Keeffe was ready to concede that her classmate was correct, because now O'Keeffe had to support herself financially. She quit art school and began drawing lace and embroidery for an advertising agency in Chicago.

After a year of illustrating advertisements, another setback occurred for O'Keeffe. When O'Keeffe contracted the measles, her eyesight was weakened to the extent that she thought she might never paint again. For six years following her illness, O'Keeffe worked as an art advisor and teacher in the public schools and community colleges of Texas and elsewhere. Although she was still able to paint, she no longer entertained the idea of becoming a recognized artist. Therefore she disregarded the lessons she was taught in art school and began painting and drawing—at the suggestion of a mentor, Arthur Wesley Dow—self-expressive abstract pictures that emerged out of her own soul.

O'Keeffe was content to create artwork for her own amusement and that of her friends in the early 1900s. Her friend Anita Pollitzer was not content with that. She believed that a set of charcoals, pastels, and watercolors that O'Keeffe had sent to her cried out for recognition. Without O'Keeffe's permission, Anita showed some of O'Keeffe's charcoal drawings to the director of an avant garde art gallery in New York.

O'Keeffe was angry when she soon learned through an acquaintance that ten of her private drawings were hanging on the wall of 291 Gallery. She confronted the museum's director, Alfred Stieglitz, who convinced O'Keeffe to leave the sketches on display. Stieglitz later convinced her to marry him as well.

Although over time, the O'Keeffe-Stieglitz marriage lost some of its original passion, the two artists never lost respect for each other. O'Keeffe posed for hundreds of artistic photographs taken by her husband who was not only an art critic and gallery director, but also one of the world's first professional photographers. Even after the couple began living separately, Stieglitz exhibited O'Keeffe's works annually in solo shows for nearly 30 years until his death in 1946.

Alfred Stieglitz was not the only person to appreciate the artistic genius of Georgia O'Keeffe. After marrying Stieglitz, O'Keeffe gave up teaching, moved to New York, and began painting full time. When she began painting huge, close-up views of flower blossoms—something no artist had ever done before—in 1924, the entire art world took notice. When O'Keeffe moved to New Mexico and began painting clean, original desert landscapes and an entire series of stark skull and bone paintings, even the world beyond art began to take notice. Georgia O'Keeffe was developing into a recognized painter, a major figure in American modernism.

O'Keeffe began to collect numerous prestigious awards and honors. In 1942 she accepted an honorary doctorate from the University of Wisconsin. In 1946 the New York Museum of Modern Art mounted a retrospective exhibit of her art—the first of the museum's retrospectives to feature a female artist. In 1949 she was elected to the National Institute of Arts and Letters. In 1963 she was elected to the American Academy of Arts and Letters. In 1968 a *Life* magazine article chronicled her life and work. In 1970 a retrospective exhibit in New York confirmed her standing as a world-class painter and introduced her work to a whole new generation. In 1977 she received the Presidential Medal of Honor. In 1997 The Georgia O'Keeffe Museum opened in Santa Fe, New Mexico, posthumously.

Georgia O'Keeffe lived for 98 active years. She produced enough critically acclaimed works of art to exhibit in over 20 one-woman shows and as part of the permanent collections of several important galleries. Even after she lost her central vision in 1971, she continued to paint, aided by an assistant. Additionally, while residing in New Mexico from 1937 until her death in 1986, she developed an intimate understanding of the landscapes that became her trademark, hiking the cliffs and basins of the land and growing her own vegetables in gardens within the beloved adobe compound wherein she resided. Georgia O'Keeffe once told an interviewer that she had never in her life experienced boredom. She was thankful that she experienced an inner understanding of light, color, and the artistic form, that she did understand the significance of nature and beauty, and that her friend Anita Pollitzer did understand that the world would appreciate the pure and inspired art of a woman who nearly put a childhood dream to rest.

Name ______________________________

Visualizing Beauty

Georgia O'Keeffe became known for her pure, clean landscapes and still lifes. Her close-up and enlarged views of flower blossoms and stark and lean portrayals of New York City skylines and New Mexico landscapes were neither representational nor abstract, but rather a personal, self-expressive combination of the two.

On your own paper, illustrate ~~three~~ one of the following scenes and/or still lifes using your own personal style that may combine elements of realism or abstractism. Then see if your classmates can match your drawings with the descriptions you chose to illustrate.

1. Draw a scene out of the Wild West. Include a dusty downtown main street lined with a saloon, a general store, and a church and featuring at least two cowboys, four horses, and a buggy.

2. Illustrate a wicker basket filled with fruit of all sizes, shapes, colors, and varieties.

3. Draw a close-up and enlarged view of an insect of your choice.

4. Draw a desert landscape in midday complete with sand, cacti, and a lizard.

5. Choose one element of a crowded football stadium to illustrate close-up. You may choose to draw, for example, the heads of a few of the fans in the crowd, a bandaged hand of one of the players, a hot dog dripping with mustard, a football in flight, or a single, bright, hot stadium light.

6. Illustrate an interior scene of a modern kitchen. Include large and small appliances, decorative curtains, floor tiles, and wallpaper.

7. Enlarge a few inches of a garment into a detailed drawing. Choose a small section of a seam or zipper, a single button, or a small area of a printed or textured fabric to illustrate.

8. Draw dark thunderclouds in an ominous-looking afternoon sky.

9. Draw a night scene of the stars and moon or choose a single night sky object to illustrate alone.

10. Draw a close-up view of an object from computer science such as a computer chip, a small section of a keyboard, a single icon on an opening screen, or the numerous holes of a computer's speaker unit.

Name ______________________

"Mr O'Keeffe"

Alfred Stieglitz, husband of Georgia O'Keeffe from 1924 until his death in 1946, was a giant in the American art world of the late 1800s and early 1900s. As an art critic and owner and director of several galleries in New York City, Stieglitz launched the American modernism movement by promoting and exhibiting the works of such painters as Georgia O'Keeffe, Marsden Hartley, and John Marin.

As an influential photographer of simple and sincere photos, Stieglitz also urged the development of photography as an art form. He founded and edited periodicals of photography, founded and directed a national organization of photographers, lectured and lobbied for the acceptance of photography in the art world, and exhibited the works of photographic greats including Edward Steichen and Ansel Adams.

Use an encyclopedia or reference book to help you match the artists whom Stieglitz promoted that are listed in the box with their descriptions below.

MARSDEN HARTLEY	JOHN MARIN	ANSEL ADAMS
EDWARD STEICHEN	HENRI MATISSE	PABLO PICASSO
ARTHUR DOVE	PAUL CÉZANNE	HENRI ROUSSEAU
AUGUSTE RODIN		

______________ 1. The work of this French sculptor who used texture and modeling to express emotion in such works as *The Thinker* was first introduced to an American audience at a Stieglitz gallery.

______________ 2. This American watercolorist, known especially for his series of Maine seascapes, first showed his work to the public at Stieglitz's 291 Gallery.

______________ 3. This American artist who served as the chief photographer for *Vanity Fair* and *Vogue* magazines co-owned the 291 Gallery with Alfred Stieglitz. Later he directed the Museum of Modern Art, where he prepared a photographic exhibit called "The Family Man" that toured the world and sold 3 million copies in book form.

______________ 4. In a small gallery in New York City, Stieglitz staged the first one-man shows of these two famous European modern artists—
______________ the Spaniard known for his cubist paintings and sculptures and considered the twentieth century's greatest artist, and the Frenchman famous for his use of flat designs and bold colors.

______________ 5. Stieglitz's galleries often displayed the American west landscapes and other sharply focused works of this famous photographer.

______________ 6. Stieglitz was the first to bring exhibits of these two European
______________ painters to American galleries.

______________ 7. Works of this first American abstract artist including *Rise of the Full Moon* were often displayed in Stieglitz galleries.

______________ 8. Paintings of this European-influenced American painter, including *Lobster Fishermen,* hung in Stieglitz's galleries near the end of Stieglitz's life when this artist was just coming into form.

American Ambassador of Jazz

Background

At the beginning of the twentieth century, New Orleans gave birth to a new musical genre. Laden with solid rhythms drummed out by percussion instruments and repeated chord progressions played by a piano or bass, the new sound used written scores only as general guides on which brass instrumentalists established musical improvisations. Jazz music evolved out of the early black American experience. West African music, black American folk songs, black brass band marches, Negro spirituals, blues, hymns, and minstrel show banjo music all contributed to the new all-American genre.

Originally played by small marching bands or solo pianists at weddings, funerals, parades, picnics, and Mardi Gras celebrations, jazz was being performed in clubs by the first decade of the 1900s and released on record albums by the 1920s. As it grew, jazz branched into many variations including New Orleans jazz, Dixieland, New York jazz, swing, and bebop.

Although each subdivision of jazz claims its own sound, they all share certain characteristics. Jazz music makes use of slides and nuances in pitch. It features syncopated rhythms in which stress is placed on normally weak beats. The pulse of jazz music swings. Jazz thrives on the understanding that a single chord progression established early in a piece can yield an infinite number of improvised melodies when repeated again and again.

In this lesson students read about the early life difficulties of one of the most influential musicians of the jazz era. The impoverished Louis Armstrong grew into a jazz legend, demonstrating to students that early challenges and mistakes do not prohibit future success.

Teaching Activities

All That Jazz: Students distinguish among several distinctive styles of jazz.
Jazz Greats: Students research the lives of famous jazz musicians and share their findings with classmates.

Extensions

1. Experiment with stream-of-consciousness writing, the literary equivalent of musical improvisation.
2. Research the history of the instruments of jazz including the cornet, trumpet, saxophone, trombone, tuba, snare drum, bass, and clarinet. What other musical genres throughout history have made use of each instrument?
3. Listen to jazz recordings in your classroom. Challenge students to identify individual instruments in a single recording. Attempt to distinguish specific styles or artists when playing a number of separate recordings.
4. Invite members of your class who play musical instruments to entertain their classmates with improvised tunes.
5. Challenge your students to nonsense-syllable scat singing based on a popular tune.
6. Require students to sketch jazz instruments on drawing paper and write captions describing the instruments. Display drawings on a classroom bulletin board.
7. Locate e-mail addresses of jazz musicians and write electronic letters of gratitude for the contributions jazz has made to all modern genres of music.

American Ambassador of Jazz

Eleven-year-old Louis Daniel Armstrong got a bit carried away in celebrating the arrival of the new year on January 1, 1913. At that early age, he was already accustomed to living a somewhat out-of-control life on the streets. Raised by a loving, but impoverished mother, who earned a meager living cleaning houses, and a grandmother who looked out for the boy when his mother enjoyed the night life of New Orleans, Louis grew up fast. His father had abandoned the family shortly after Louis's birth, and the Storyville section of early twentieth-century New Orleans was a challenging place for a boy to grow up without a father. By fifth grade the child had already stopped attending school. Rather than taking tests and reading textbooks, Louis's early memories were of a street life that included witnessing shoot-outs and stabbings and participating in fistfights, garbage can raids, street-side harmonizing with makeshift musical groups for handouts, and frequent run-ins with local police officers.

During an outdoor New Year's party in 1913, Louis went too far. He shot a gun into the air in celebration of the arrival of the new year. The New Orleans police department was not amused. Louis Armstrong was sentenced to two years incarceration in the city's Colored Waifs' Home. The sentence must have seemed unfortunate at the time, but jazz lovers today can be grateful it was issued.

Peter Davis, the music instructor at the home, taught young Louis Armstrong the basics of music while he was there. He trained Louis to sing, play the drums, and blow a bugle and cornet. He enlisted the talented youngster in the Colored Waifs' Home band. Louis Armstrong would be forever in debt to Mr. Davis.

At 14 Louis was released onto the streets of New Orleans again. For the sake of survival, he sold newspapers and coal and helped unload boats that landed in the harbor, but he now knew his ultimate fate included music. In the evenings after getting off work, Louis spent hours listening to bands play in clubs throughout New Orleans. He especially liked the music of King Oliver, and King especially liked the enthusiasm of the boy. Mr. Oliver gave Louis a cornet of his own and acted as a musical mentor to the boy. Louis did not let Mr. Oliver down. In fact, he far exceeded his tutor in talent and—eventually—success.

By the time he was 16, Louis had formed a band of his own that performed in dive bars throughout New Orleans. By 1919 Louis was playing with King Oliver's band on days when he was not traveling up and down the Mississippi performing with a riverboat band. When King Oliver left Kid Ory's band, he recommended Louis take his place. Later, Mr. Oliver sent for Louis to play with him in Chicago.

Before his twenty-fifth birthday, Louis Armstrong found that his cornet- and trumpet-playing skills were in demand with bands all over the East and Midwest. He played in New York, Chicago, St. Louis, and New Orleans. He played as a member of famous orchestras and individually accompanied the vocal performances of well-known blues singers both in live shows and on recordings.

In 1924 Louis Armstrong broke out on his own. With the help of his second wife who became one of its members, he formed a band called Louis Armstrong's Hot Five. The group never performed live but recorded some of the most enduring sounds in jazz. Later, when he began to record music with an electrical rather than an acoustical method, he added a drummer and tuba player to form the Hot Seven. Jazz music would never be the same.

Louis Armstrong reformed jazz from a collective improvisational experience to a soloist's art form. His virtuosity playing the trumpet, impressive conducting, impassioned style of singing, and ever-present smile and grace earned Armstrong a place in the hearts of Americans. His relaxed attitude in the studio earned him a place in history. During a recording session in which he was singing "Heebie Jeebies," his sheet music fell to the floor. Unflustered, Louis began to sing random syllables, giving birth to "scat singing."

That would not be the only time Louis Armstrong made history. In 1932 Armstrong became the first jazz musician to tour throughout Europe. Before his life ended, he had entertained people all around the globe. He became known as the father of swing and the unofficial American Musical Ambassador to the World. His talents and immense popularity landed Louis Armstrong the position of the first black American to host a weekly radio program, gained him a role in over 50 feature films, and provided him countless hits, awards, and earnings. In 1963, when the 62-year-old's award-winning "Hello Dolly" knocked the Beatles out of the number one slot on the pop charts, Louis Armstrong's talents and popularity even earned him the world record for oldest man to win a Grammy Award.

Mr. Armstrong's gravelly heart-felt vocals and virtuosic trumpet solos continue to entertain and influence audiences and musicians some 30 years after his death. "Potato Head Blues," "Cornet Chop Suey," and "What a Wonderful World" are still heard on the soundtracks of countless motion pictures, and his musical influence continues to flow from the voices and instruments of musicians of nearly every genre. The little boy who grew up without a male role model of his own became a symbol of hard work, happiness, grace, style, and talent to generations of boys and girls—as well as men and women—around the world. Louis Armstrong had showmanship, a unique sense of rhythm, outstanding abilities in musical spontaneity and improvisation, and awe-inspiring mastery over the trumpet. These talents coupled with the playing of high register notes previously assumed unattainable made Armstrong the very definition of jazz.

Name ______________________________

All That Jazz

As jazz music grew and developed in the early years of the twentieth century, it branched into distinctive subdivisions. Use an encyclopedia or other reference materials to help you distinguish one jazz style from another. Define each in a complete sentence. You may find some styles overlap in their descriptions even in encyclopedia articles.

1. New Orleans Jazz ______________________________
2. Dixieland ______________________________
3. Chicago Style ______________________________
4. Modal Jazz ______________________________
5. Fusion Jazz ______________________________
6. New York Jazz ______________________________
7. Swing ______________________________
8. Bebop ______________________________
9. Third Stream ______________________________
10. Jazz Revival ______________________________
11. Cool ______________________________

Now compare and constrast two styles that overlap.

____

Now write about a performer who became well-known for success in more than one style.

____

Name ______________________________

Jazz Greats

Research and write a two- to three-page report about the personal life and musical accomplishments of one of the performers listed below. Share your findings with your classmates by delivering a speech and—if possible—playing a piece of music recorded by the artist you chose.

DUKE ELLINGTON is considered the greatest composer in jazz history. He wrote over 2,000 musical scores and directed bands in over 20,000 concerts in 65 nations.

HERBIE HANCOCK made his first professional showing as a pianist at the age of 11 when he played with the Chicago Symphony Orchestra. He became a pioneer of fusion jazz, but also played bebop and modal jazz and wrote the scores to several movie sound tracks. In 1980 he formed a rap group called the Rocket Band. In 1996 he produced a record that set modern pop songs to jazz improvisational scores.

JOHN COLTRANE was a tenor saxophonist and composer who became a leader in free form jazz when he abandoned tonality, wrote complex harmonies into his music, and intentionally made his instrument scream and moan.

MILES DAVIS was a trumpet player and bandleader who worked in bebop, fusion, and cool jazz. He played in bands from the time he was 15 years old and had a thorough education in classical music. His smooth expressive style earned him 12 Grammy Awards over the course of his lifetime.

CHICK COREA began playing the piano at the age of four. He became a famous crossover pianist who could play classical, bebop, fusion, and New Orleans jazz.

BESSIE SMITH, the Empress of the Blues, recorded numerous albums with such famous jazz musicians as Louis Armstrong and Benny Goodman. Her rich, deep voice made her the most popular blues singer of her day and a legend today.

ELLA FITZGERALD, a legendary blues singer who was discovered at a talent show in Harlem, became famous for her ability to scat sing. She sang with many jazz musicians and toured successfully all over the world.

BENNY GOODMAN, a legendary clarinetist and orchestra leader, began playing professionally at age 14. By the time he reached his twenties, he had his own weekly radio program. Known as the "King of Swing," Benny also starred in motion pictures and performed classical music.

"Hello, I'm Johnny Cash"

Background

Country and western music has its roots in blues, black rural dance tunes, and the old-time music of the southern Appalachians. For generations the banjo-supported sounds of hillbilly bands could be heard stompin' out rhythms up and down the Mississippi, but the true birthday of country music was not until August 1, 1927. On that date Ralph Peer of Victor Records signed on a solo artist named Jimmie Rodgers and a singing group called the Carter Family. Rodgers, later dubbed the "Father of Country Music," popularized sentimental ballads and old Southern standards to the sound of a mandolin, a guitar, three banjos, and yodeling vocals. The Carter Family astounded the nation with beautifully harmonized Appalachian sounds.

By the late 1930s country music was a mainstay to a sector of the nation that clamored to the down-home tunes rooted in the history of America. Roy Acuff, the "King of Country Music," transformed the Grand Ole Opry from a place where part-time performers promoted their live shows on a Saturday night radio broadcast to a country music institution that professionalized the genre.

Country and western music of the 1930s and 1940s branched beyond the original Appalachian sounds of its originators. Stars like Roy Rogers and Gene Autry, who used dry wit, cowboy skills, and talents in both music and acting to land their names in both Western movie credits and on record labels, welcomed in an era of Cowboy Music. At the same time large bands, complete with horns and strings, introduced the sound of Western swing. Meanwhile, groups like the Blue Grass Boys offered bluegrass hits while Hank Williams popularized the honky-tonk style.

By the 1950s country and western music was making the best of contemporary technology. Records from that era featured the smooth voices of stars like Patsy Cline and Jim Reeves singing crossover hits on polished and artistically produced albums.

Then came Johnny Cash. Johnny's deep baritone voice, gritty themes, and sincere style that relied on nothing more than a voice and guitar gave rise to country rock or outlaw country. He and a few of his fellow "outlaws" became country music legends, but it was a challenging road from birth to legend for Johnny Cash.

In this lesson students read about the failures and successes of a man who maintains that obstacles and challenges serve well to strengthen a man on his way to better things.

Teaching Activities

Country Music Legends: Students learn the histories of other country music stars.
Sharing the Wealth: Students learn of the charitable actions of a man who has experienced his share of challenges.

Extensions

1. Share Johnny Cash recordings with students during an appropriate class period.
2. As an alternative to the writing of poems, encourage students to write song lyrics either to original tunes or to already familiar melodies.
3. Organize a musical talent show in which student musicians from your class or school perform for the school or community.
4. Assign comparative reports on various music genres.
5. Require students to write a review of a concert they attend in person or watch on TV.
6. Promote student attendance at school or local choral and band performances.

Student Reading

"Hello, I'm Johnny Cash"

In 1936 a four-year-old boy listened to a song called "Hobo Bill's Last Ride" play on an old Victrola. At that moment, the child knew he too would record albums. What he did not know is that he would live 19 challenging years before realizing his dream.

Johnny Cash was born to poverty-stricken sharecroppers in Kingsland, Arkansas. When he was three years old, he accompanied his family on a move to Dyess Colony at the invitation of the United States government, which offered farmers struggling through the Great Depression cash incentives to relocate. For the next 15 years, Johnny went to school in the fall and winter months and picked cotton alongside his parents and siblings in the summers. As do many Great Depression survivors, he remembers months of going without "extras" and not eating enough to fill his stomach at countless meals. When Johnny's mother noticed a talent and desire to sing in her son, she had to take in laundry from local school teachers in addition to her duties picking cotton to earn enough money for her son to attend private lessons. Fatefully, Johnny's voice teacher worked with Johnny only once or twice before suggesting to the boy that he quit lessons and keep his own marvelous and unique style. Johnny Cash never forgot the sacrifices of his mother or the words of the teacher who had faith in his sound.

By the time he graduated from high school, national economic conditions had greatly improved, and Johnny was able to secure a job at an automobile plant in Detroit. A few months later, news of the Korean War prompted Johnny to enlist in the United States Air Force. While serving Uncle Sam at his assigned station in Germany, Johnny Cash was a busy man. In addition to completing his military duties, Johnny bought his first guitar and taught himself to play it, formed a band called the Barbarians that played in nightclubs near his base, and contributed poetry to a military newspaper. Meanwhile his childhood dream never left Johnny's mind.

When his term in the Air Force ended, Johnny moved to Memphis, Tennessee. While enrolled in radio announcers' school and employed as a door-to-door appliance salesman, Johnny pounded recording studio doors, too. Finally, Sam Phillips of Sun Records responded to his knocking. Annoyed at the young man's persistent phone calls and appearances at his studio, he at last consented to listen to Johnny sing. Mr. Phillips liked what he heard. So did the general public. Johnny's first single "Hey Porter" and its flip side "Cry, Cry, Cry" were local hits; and his next release, "Folsom Prison Blues," became a number four national country music billboard smash.

It seemed hard times were over for the son of the Arkansas sharecroppers. He began starring in a national weekly radio program. He was engaged in an intensive touring schedule. He performed at the prestigious Grand Ole Opry. He was picked up by Columbia Records, a major label. He was asked to host a television variety show. Each song he recorded following "Folsom Prison Blues" seemed to do better on the charts than the one before.

Still hard times were not over for Johnny Cash. The 300 shows he performed each year took their toll on "The Man in Black." Johnny Cash began popping pills to provide himself with energy. For ten long years he struggled with a severe drug and alcohol addiction. He was arrested and jailed seven times for narcotic offenses, drunk and disorderly charges, and related crimes.

When he finally escaped his addictions, Johnny Cash used the lessons he learned from his mistakes to the benefit of others. He began performing concerts in prison settings and supporting ex-cons in their efforts to reenter society. He wrote a religious novel and starred in a movie about the Christian faith, which he credited with helping him overcome his addictions. His first-hand knowledge of hardships and poverty added a remarkable sincerity to his songs, which impressed and entertained millions.

Then hardship struck again. In 1986 Columbia Records chose not to renew his contract. Country music had evolved into a sound that no longer seemed to have a place for the deep and unique tones of Johnny Cash. Even when American Recordings signed on Johnny Cash in 1994, country music radio stations around the nation chose not to play his new songs.

Regardless of the country radio stations' refusal to welcome Johnny Cash back, the critics appreciated his new efforts. Both his 1994 CD entitled *American Recordings* and his 1998 work *Unchained* earned him Grammy Awards, the latter for Best Country Album of the Year. In all, Johnny Cash holds ten Grammy Awards including a 1999 Lifetime Achievement Award. He has been inducted into the Country Music Hall of Fame, the Rock and Roll Hall of Fame, and the Songwriter's Hall of Fame. He has produced 130 billboard country hits at the rate of two or more chart singles per year for 38 consecutive years. He has influenced and/or performed with artists across the board from grunge rockers to modern country stars. Over 100 groups have recorded their own version of his immensely popular "I Walk the Line." In addition to singing and writing hit songs, he has starred in movies and television programs, written two autobiographies and a novel, and contributed time, talent, and financial support to causes from prison reform to cancer research.

As he approaches age 70, Johnny Cash battles his latest hardship, Shy-Drager Syndrome—a Parkinson's-like disease—with the same grace and sincerity with which he has faced all of life's challenges. When a 1997 performance was interrupted by the shaking caused by his disease, Johnny Cash openly informed his audience of his medical condition. Never one to hide his mistakes or misfortunes, Johnny Cash is a success because of his honest faith in what he does and who he is.

Name ____________________

Country Music Legends

Johnny Cash is only one of a number of musicians who have paved the way for today's country and western sound. Read about some of the others below and then create a quiz about the information on your own paper. Your quiz may include multiple-choice, fill-in-the-blank, and/or true-and-false questions. When you have completed writing your exam, trade it with the exam of another student and see if you can pass each other's test.

THE CARTER FAMILY—which consisted of a husband and wife, a cousin, and a number of others—was producing its Appalachian harmonies at the beginning of country music history in the early 1920s. As group members' children grew up, they joined the Carter Family musical group, too. Eventually, the younger generation made up the entire group. One of the younger generation Carters, June, became Johnny Cash's wife in 1968.

JIMMY RODGERS, considered "the Father of Country Music," worked on the railroad for many years before becoming the first country star to sign with Victor Records. He was known for his ballads and yodeling tunes.

ROY ACUFF, "the King of Country Music," was a minor league baseball player whose sports career was cut short by a severe case of sunstroke. So he turned to a music career in which he popularized the Grand Ole Opry, contributed such classic country hits as the "Wabash Cannonball," and produced the music of a number of country music greats.

ROY ROGERS incorporated music, humor, and acting into his long and illustrious career that allowed him to star in over 100 western movies and television shows while recording cowboy music for a number of big-name record labels as a solo artist and a member of various groups including the Sons of the Pioneers.

THE HIGHWAYMEN was a group of country music legends including Johnny Cash, Willie Nelson, Waylon Jennings, and Kris Kristofferson who got together to release a massively successful album in 1985.

CHET ATKINS is considered by musicians of all genres to be one of the greatest guitar players of all time.

HANK WILLIAMS used the money he won in a songwriting contest at the age of 12 to form his own band and travel across the country until his untimely drug- and alcohol-related death 18 years later. Hank Williams was an immensely popular performer who introduced the honky-tonk era and attitude. In his first performance at the Grand Ole Opry, Hank was persuaded to play six encores. Many of Hank Williams' 100+ songs continue to be popular today.

MERLE HAGGARD, a legend of outlaw country music, spent a number of childhood years during the Great Depression living out of a railroad boxcar. As a young man, Merle found himself frequently in trouble with the law. In 1958, while residing in the San Quentin Penitentiary, Merle Haggard watched one of Johnny Cash's famous prison concerts and was inspired to make a success of his own music abilities when he was released from prison two years later.

GRAND OLE OPRY

Name ______________________________

Sharing the Wealth

Johnny Cash has dedicated time, talent, and money to a number of causes that are close to his heart. Tell about personal experiences from the life of Johnny Cash that might have prompted him to support the causes mentioned below. The first one has been done for you as it relies on a fact that was not included in the student reading.

1. Johnny Cash endowed a *burn research center*. Why? Johnny Cash's guitarist of many years, Luther Perkins, died in a fire.

2. Johnny Cash supports the YWCA. Why? ______________________________

   ____

3. Johnny Cash campaigns for prison reform, writes letters to inmates, performs for prisoners, and assists ex-cons in reentering society. Why? ______________________

   ____

4. Johnny Cash supports numerous women's shelters around the country. Why? ______

   ____

5. Johnny Cash financially encourages groups, such as Campus Life, that support young Christians. Why? ____

   ____

6. Johnny Cash plays benefits for Native Americans. Why? ______________________

   ____

7. Johnny Cash supports mental health organizations. Why? ____________________

   ____

If you had money or talents to contribute to charitable organizations or social causes, which would you support? Why? ______________________________________

____

____

____

____

____

____

Sly Guy

Background

The motion picture industry has never been especially accepting of artistic individualism. From 1901 until 1912, when movies were first being produced, everything from a film's subject matter to its length was dictated by a trust of leading producers called the Motion Picture Patents Company. Following the disintegration of that group, Hollywood studios controlled all aspects of moviemaking.

From 1915 until the mid-1960s, movies were made from start to finish by large and profitable individual studios which staffed their own writers, directors, actors, and craftspeople. All studio employees were held to tight contracts, which severely limited their artistic freedom. Writers wrote only screenplays they were assigned to write. Directors and actors worked only with scripts they were told to work with. Editors, costume designers, and cinematographers were tied to the studio that employed them.

Even after a number of successful writers, directors, and actors broke free from the artistically restrictive studio system to create their own organization called United Artists, the movie industry continued to largely ignore artistic genius in favor of recognizable stars and proven-profitable screenplay themes. Although motion picture performers and craftspeople increasingly became "free agents" beginning in the mid-1960s, moviemaking did not cease to be an "insiders" game. The throngs of men and women who flocked to the now-public screen tests did not bring so many new faces to the screen, as it did more charitable organizations to the city of Hollywood in an attempt to meet the needs of its rapidly growing population of "starving artists."

Enter Sylvester Stallone, a B-movie actor with an irresistible screenplay and a deaf ear for the word "no." In this lesson students learn how a troubled youth grew into a determined young man whose refusal to compromise landed him in the eventual position of fame and fortune.

Teaching Activities

Access Denied: Students learn of the pre-Hollywood lives of some actors and actresses and then imagine the careers of famous actors and actresses had they not become successful in Hollywood.
Hollywood History: Students learn of the fascinating history of Tinseltown and moviemaking.

Extensions

1. Assign the writing of movie reviews of a Sylvester Stallone movie.
2. Assign reports on the pre-Hollywood lives of famous actors and actresses.
3. Assign reports on the various jobs in the film industry.
4. Offer opportunities for students to perform in role-play skits, full-length plays, and other dramas.
5. As a class, attend a live theatrical performance.
6. Assign the writing of a paper comparing and contrasting movies, books, and plays.
7. Create a class book of reviews of family movies.
8. Research and report on the interconnected histories of photography, filmmaking, and the scientific study of motion observation.

Sly Guy

On July 6, 1946, in the Hell's Kitchen District of Manhattan, a boy was being born when a forceps accident severed a nerve in the infant's face. As a result, Sylvester Stallone was left with a permanently drooping lower lip, a crooked left eye, and a partially paralyzed tongue. For the future portrayer of the fictional boxer Rocky Balboa, that was Round One.

Round Two was not any more pleasant. Young Stallone was a sickly child who suffered through rickets and countless childhood ailments that made him the recipient of much teasing and ridicule. All the while, he bounced from home to home and school to school. Because his parents were constantly struggling, both financially and as a couple, Stallone spent most of his first five years in foster care. Following his parents' divorce in 1957, the child lived unhappily first with his father and then with his mother.

His tense childhood prompted Stallone to act out negatively. During his teen years he was kicked out of a dozen schools. His grades were poor, his friends were few, and he was voted by his classmates, "most likely to end up in the electric chair." Although it must not have seemed like it at the time, arguably the best thing that ever happened to the boy was that he wound up in a special high school for emotionally disturbed youth. While there, he played in sports, acted in school plays, and raised his grades enough to land himself in a college in Switzerland following graduation.

Acting in a school play in college inspired Sylvester Stallone to make performing his life's work, but Round Three might have dissuaded a less determined man. Once he returned to the United States, Stallone found that his deep voice, slurred speech, and peculiar appearance qualified him for only minor roles in off-Broadway plays and quirky B-movies. When he was turned down for a part in *The Godfather*, Sylvester turned to writing scripts.

Stallone sold several screenplays while continuing to act in moderately successful films until the mid-1970s. Then he wrote a Cinderella story about a down-and-out boxer who makes good. Stallone was convinced not only that the screenplay could be made into a successful movie, but that the leading role was the ideal medium for his own acting style.

Sylvester Stallone beat the pavement and knocked down doors in Hollywood. At studio after studio, movie producers gave the same response: "Fantastic script. We'll pay top dollar. No, you can't play the leading role. We need a star." At studio after studio, Sylvester Stallone gave the same response: "No thank you."

Finally, he was rewarded for his patience. Producers Irwin Winkler and Robert Chartoff of United Artists agreed to make the movie with Stallone playing the role of Rocky Balboa. Still they did not intend to take a blind leap off a towering cliff. They would commit no more than one million dollars to the project.

Sylvester Stallone was undaunted by the movie's small budget. He enlisted the help of family members and Hollywood friends to put the show together. *Rocky* was produced on a shoestring, filmed with no big-name stars, and marketed only on a low level; but Stallone had done what he set out to do. He had turned his script into a movie and himself into a leading man.

The enormous and unexpected success of the low-budget, no-big-name-movie-stars film mirrored the miracle in *Rocky's* storyline. The film earned back 60 times what it cost to produce. It spurred on the production of four sequels. It claimed three Academy Awards including one for 1976's Best Picture. And it catapulted Sylvester Stallone into stardom as both an actor and a screenplay writer.

Sylvester Stallone has acted, directed, and produced and/or written over 50 films. Four of his movies earned over 100 million dollars at the box office. Rocky and Rambo, whom he both created and portrayed, have become established characters in American culture. The young boy who was injured and sickly from birth, tossed from home to home, kicked out of 12 schools, and voted "most likely to end up in the electric chair," turned the tables on fate. His determination to succeed in the field of his choice turned his own personal life into the same rags-to-riches style story as that of the now-hailed Rocky Balboa.

Name ______________________________

Access Denied

Part A: Sylvester Stallone was not the only movie star who was slow to gain his position of fame. Many of the movie stars you see acting on the cinema screen today did not seem destined for stardom in early life. Use a book of Hollywood trivia, the Web site 4trivia.4anything.com, or any number of trivia sites that appear when you search for "Hollywood Trivia" on any search engine to help you match the following famous names listed on the left with the pre-Hollywood facts about each listed on the right.

______ 1. Cher	A. Worked as a hairdresser at his sister's salon
______ 2. Adam Sandler	B. Was expelled from high school for hitting a teacher
______ 3. Tom Cruise	C. Worked as a coffin polisher
______ 4. Danny Glover	D. Suffered severe child abuse
______ 5. W. C. Fields	E. Sold Mouseketeer ears at Disneyland
______ 6. Danny DeVito	F. Stuttered until he joined the drama club in high school
______ 7. Brad Pitt	G. Was told by acting teacher to choose a different trade
______ 8. Cary Grant	H. Worked as a juggler in the circus
______ 9. Oprah Winfrey	I. Wore giant chicken costume for fast-foods chain
______ 10. Steve Martin	J. Worked for the Canadian post office
______ 11. Dan Aykroyd	K. As a dyslexic was unable to read until age 18
______ 12. Richard Pryor	L. Was a high school dropout
______ 13. Bruce Willis	M. Turned to acting in high school when injured in sports
______ 14. Sean Connery	N. Was employed as a social worker
______ 15. Dustin Hoffman	O. Among other jobs, worked as a waiter

Part B: Now imagine the following big names in Hollywood were denied access to movie acting for whatever reason. If they were not actors, what job might each person be good at and why?

1. Drew Barrymore would be a good ______________________ because she ____.
2. Mike Myers would be a good ______________________ because he ____.
3. Neve Campbell would be a good ______________________ because she ____.
4. Will Smith would be a good ______________________ because he ____.
5. Lisa Kudrow would be a good ______________________ because she ____.
6. Jennifer Love Hewitt would be a good ______________________ because she ____.
7. Leonardo DiCaprio would be a good ______________________ because he ____.

Name ____________________

Hollywood History

Use an encyclopedia or other reference book to help you determine which of the following statements about the history of Hollywood and filmmaking are true. Write true or false in the space provided to indicate your response.

________ 1. The motion picture industry developed out of a scientific interest in the eye's ability to perceive motion.

________ 2. A forerunner to motion pictures was the zoetrope, a revolving drum on which still pictures were mounted and spun.

________ 3. The *kinescope*, the original motion picture machine, was invented by Thomas Edison.

________ 4. The first films told elaborate stories of love and mysterious intrigue.

________ 5. The first real narrative films were produced by a magician.

________ 6. The first major American film was called *The Great Plane Robbery.*

________ 7. One of the first silent movie actors to become famous was an ancestor of Drew Barrymore.

________ 8. The first true American motion picture masterpiece, called *Birth of a Nation*, was a controversial film because it sympathetically portrayed western gunfighters.

________ 9. The first motion picture studio to open in Hollywood did so in 1911.

________ 10. Prior to 1945, the Hollywood sign read "Hollywoodland."

________ 11. The Hollywood sign was originally displayed to advertise a department store.

________ 12. Today's all-steel Hollywood sign which cost donors $27,700 per letter to construct was unveiled on Hollywood's seventy-fifth anniversary in 1978.

________ 13. The studio system that dominated moviemaking until the mid-1960s allowed studios to choose the movies actors would act in.

________ 14. The names of actors and actresses did not appear in the credits of early movies.

________ 15. The first sound film, which came out in 1927, was titled *The Jazz Singer.*

________ 16. Popular genres of early films included Westerns, slapstick comedies, and romantic melodramas.

________ 17. The first internationally renowned movie star was Rudolph Valentino.

________ 18. During the early 1940s many men and women who worked in radio moved over to movie jobs.

________ 19. The 1939 film *The Wizard of Oz* was the first motion picture to be produced in Technicolor.

________ 20. Wide-screen productions and 3-D movies were produced in an attempt to win back audiences who turned to television following World War II.

The Sultan of Swat

Background

A famous American myth names Abner Doubleday as the Father of Modern Baseball. Although little evidence supports this claim that the American Civil War Union officer devised the diamond-shaped field or the sport's modern playing positions, professional baseball clearly is an American invention. Most historians agree on a story something like this . . .

Stick and ball contests had been played for fun—and as part of ceremonies—since ancient times. Gradually, ancient Greek and Egyptian games evolved into more organized sports played in Europe during the Middle Ages. By the early 1600s American colonists were imitating the English stick-and-ball games of cricket and rounders.

There were many American versions of rounders. The game always challenged a player to hit a ball with a stick before attempting to run around bases without being "put out" by the catching of a pop fly or the "plugging" of the runner with a ball. But specific rules, field arrangements, and names for the sport varied with locale. Town ball was a common name for the American version of rounders. So was baseball.

By the 1830s "baseball" claimed enough fans in the United States that clubs began to form in larger communities. In 1842 the Knickerbocker Base Ball Club was organized in New York City. The Knickerbocker Club made the first serious attempt to regulate the playing of baseball. The club developed a formal set of rules, defined a specific baseball field by regulating distances between plates, and established—for the first time—foul lines.

Baseball's popularity mushroomed, and the sport began to bring in revenue. By the 1850s towns and landowners charged clubs to maintain baseball fields for their use, while vendors sold snacks and drinks to the game's numerous spectators. In 1869 the first national baseball organization approved the paying of players, and the professional game was born. Fans were now excited enough about watching a game to pay admission fees.

During the next 50 years, baseball gained its foothold as America's favorite pastime. Then in 1919 seven Chicago players were banned from professional play for throwing the World Series. The sport was disgraced. Fans lost interest. Players lost respect. Professional baseball was at an all-time low until . . .

Babe Ruth took to the pitcher's mound and then to the batter's box. Besides the leadership of baseball's first commissioner, Kennesaw Mountain Landis, who brought integrity to the professional sport of baseball, only one thing saved the game during the 1920s—the unfathomable talent and remarkable personality of George Herman Ruth.

In this lesson students read about the humble beginnings of an American legend.

Teaching Activities

Batting to Beat the Babe: Students learn about other baseball heavy hitters.
Picture This: Students choose two hall of famers and create baseball cards for them.

Extensions

1. Play a baseball game: class against class, teachers against students, or parents against students.
2. Assign reports on famous baseball players and/or managers.
3. Assign the creation of math problems using baseball statistics.

The Sultan of Swat

The year was 1920. Professional baseball was at an all-time low. When the Cincinnati Reds defeated the Chicago White Sox in the previous season's World Series, it was no surprise to a handful of professional gamblers. They had bribed seven White Sox players to throw the game. When the truth came out, the seven Chicago players were banned from professional play along with a teammate who did not participate, but did know of the plan. The mistake was punished, but the public image of baseball suffered.

Then an exceptional Boston Red Sox pitcher was sold to the New York Yankees. Charmed by his contagious smile, jaded baseball fans were coaxed back to the game. Under the power of his tremendous swing, they were persuaded to stay. The public image of baseball swelled to new heights.

In 1902 no one could have guessed that a seven-year-old boy named George Ruth would one day be a baseball legend. In that year, his mother and father turned over the unruly, tobacco-chewing youngster to Father Matthias at St. Mary's Industrial School. Brother Matthias tried to tame the boy, breaking him of his habits of chewing and cussing, but George remained a surly, disrespectful child. He ran away from St. Mary's on three occasions, and was "paroled" on three others only to be returned to Matthias again by his parents who became impatient with their "incorrigible" child again.

Somehow between disciplinary lectures, Brother Matthias was able to teach George to read and write and play baseball. He learned to play baseball so well, in fact, that Brother Matthias arranged for the manager of the Baltimore Orioles to watch George Ruth play once he had reached age 19. Jack Dunn liked what he saw. He offered Ruth $600 a year to play for the Orioles. Later in the same year (1914) the big, earthy young man was traded to a rival International League team and finally to the American League's Boston Red Sox.

Ruth's left-handed throwing skills made him an instant hit. Within two season's time, the "Babe"—a nickname from his days with the Orioles when a player said of Ruth that the coach had found himself a new "babe"—became one of the best pitchers of his day. In 1916 his win-loss record stood at 23-12 and in 1917 it was 24-13. During those two seasons, the young man claimed 15 shutouts. But more remarkable was Ruth's ability to swing. He was so prone to hit home runs, in fact, that in 1918, the Red Sox modified his position. The baseball great now divided his time between pitching and outfield play. When he was able to lead the American League in home runs even while dividing his time thus, Ruth was removed from the pitcher's mound permanently. His swinging talent was too valuable. Babe Ruth had to play a position that allowed him maximum batting time.

The Red Sox coaches made a good decision. In 1919 the full-time outfielder set a new home run record of 29 home runs. In 1920 the Red Sox sold Ruth to the New York Yankees for $125,000. In 1927 he broke his own record by hitting 60 home runs in a single season. During his career, the "Sultan of Swat" led the American League in home runs for the season 12 times. In all, he belted out a total of 714 home runs.

The Great Bambino changed the face of baseball. Conservative play was out. Defensive moves were less impressive. Fans attended ball games to see hard hitters like the Babe smash baseballs over the fence. Fans attended ball games to see the Babe.

Babe Ruth became a superstar, not only because he played a phenomenal game of baseball, but also because he led a phenomenal life. All the while that he swung his bat like a machine, hitting home runs in the very direction of his predictions, he continued to be intensely human. Whatever made the seven-year-old St. Mary's student rambunctious, stayed with the adult Babe. He loved to eat and drink and make merry. One time he ate so many hot dogs and drank so many sodas in one sitting that the resulting indigestion landed him in the hospital. Another time, he carried a $15,000 endorsement check from a cereal company around in his pocket for so long that it was not cashable by the time he took it to the bank. He smashed up fast expensive cars as quickly as he bought them. He held loud arguments with his team's owners over the terms of his annual contracts. His roommate on the road said that he did not room with Babe, but with his suitcase.

The Babe hid none of the sometimes embarrassing stories of his fast life from the press. In fact, he basked in his popularity. In every town and every ball field, he showered his fans with smiles and waves. One teammate suggested that Babe Ruth never in his life refused to give an autograph. When a 13-year-old Babe Ruth fan was hospitalized in New Jersey, Babe visited him before an upcoming game and promised to hit a home run for the youngster. He made good on his promise.

Eventually, Babe Ruth slowed down. He married Claire Hodgson and fathered two daughters. He became the Boston Braves' assistant manager and vice president. He left the playing field and entered the Baseball Hall of Fame as one of its original five inductees.

Younger players took over the playing field, but they could not capture the spotlight. When Babe Ruth died of throat cancer at age 53 in 1948, millions of fans paid their respects at the Yankee Stadium—"the house that Ruth built"—where his body lie in state for 26 hours. President Truman told the nation, "A whole generation of boys now grown to men will mourn the passing of the home run king of the baseball world." An Associated Press story reporting on how Babe Ruth saved baseball from the 1919 "Black Sox" scandal reported:

> The big happy-go-lucky Bambino was more than a diamond star. He was a symbol, the personification of everything that was great and spectacular in the game. He had an indefinable something called color, an inborn instinct to make every act and every move exciting.

Not a bad tribute to the man who developed out of an incorrigible, tobacco-chewing, foul-mouthed, disrespectful seven-year-old whom his parents refused to raise.

Name ____________________

Batting to Beat the Babe

Babe Ruth's 20-year career of slamming home runs motivated a long string of power hitters to try to break his many records, especially his 1927 single season record of 60 home runs. Use a baseball reference book or the Internet to help you identify the following men who approached, reached, or exceeded Babe Ruth's home run records.

LOU GEHRIG	KEN GRIFFEY, JR.	JIMMIE FOXX	HANK AARON
JOE DIMAGGIO	ROGER MARIS	SAMMY SOSA	HANK GREENBERG
HACK WILSON	MARK MCGWIRE	ROGERS HORNSBY	ERNIE BANKS
WILLIE MAYS			

__________ 1. This St. Louis player, nicknamed "Big Mac," broke Roger Maris's 1961 single-season record of 61 hits in 1998, finishing the season with the new world record of 70 home runs.

__________ 2. This Yankees' player claimed the league's batting championship twice and set a 56-consecutive-game-successful-batting-streak record during his career in which he amassed 361 homers.

__________ 3. This man who played from 1921 through 1925 had a batting average that exceeded .400. He later coached, managed, and announced professional baseball.

__________ 4. This New York Yankee was the first player to beat Babe Ruth's single-season home-run record when he hit 61 homers in 1961.

__________ 5. This Chicago Cub shared the *Sports Illustrated* Sportsman of the Year title with Mark McGwire in 1998 when he hit 66 home runs in a single season.

__________ 6. This teammate of Babe Ruth's was nicknamed "Iron Horse." He played in 2,130 consecutive games from 1925 to 1939.

__________ 7. This late-1950s power-hitting shortstop nicknamed Mr. Cub hit 47 home runs one season and 20 or more in each of 13 seasons.

__________ 8. As a Seattle Mariner he approached Roger Maris's single-season home-run record in two consecutive years, hitting 56 homers in both 1997 and 1998.

__________ 9. This Chicago Cub held the National League record of most home runs hit in a season (56 in 1930) for 68 years.

__________ 10. In 1938 this three-time major league home run leader came within three runs of beating Babe Ruth's 1927 record of 60 homers.

__________ 11. From 1929–1940 this "right-handed Babe" hit 30 or more runs every season. His highest total for a single season was 58.

__________ 12. This player's total of 660 home runs is surpassed only by the totals of Babe Ruth and Hank Aaron.

__________ 13. Nicknamed "The Hammer," this man broke Babe Ruth's career home-run record by smashing 715 homers from 1954 to 1976.

Name ______________________________

Picture This

Select two of the Baseball Hall of Famers listed here to research. Then create baseball cards for those two players in the frames below. In the frames on the left, draw pictures of the players you selected. In the frames on the right, list some interesting baseball statistics you discovered about the players you selected.

JOHNNY BENCH	YOGI BERRA	JACKIE ROBINSON	BILLY WILLIAMS
ROBERTO CLEMENTE	HARMON KILLEBREW	TED WILLIAMS	WILLIE STARGELL
MICKEY MANTLE	REGGIE JACKSON	BROOKS ROBINSON	AL LOPEZ
PEE WEE REESE	BOBBY WALLACE		

Disproving White Supremacy

Background

Track-and-field contests, which challenge athletes to run, jump, and throw objects, have a long—yet disrupted—history. Discus and javelin throwing, foot racing, and broad jumping were among the events contested at the original Olympic Games held annually in Athens, Greece, for centuries beginning in 776 B.C. After the Olympic Games were abolished by the Roman emperor Theodosius I, however, recorded history describes no organized track-and-field competitions for more than 800 years. England, at last, revived the sport during the twelfth century A.D.

Modern track-and-field contests can be traced back to the establishment of the Amateur Athletic Club in England in 1866. The club, later renamed the Amateur Athletic Association, has conducted annual national championship meets throughout Great Britain since that date. The New York Athletic Club, formed in 1868, was the first national track-and-field organization in the United States. Today, track and field is an international sport, governed by the International Amateur Athletic Federation, which approves world records and establishes standard rules for the sport. The epitome of track-and-field contests is once again the Olympic Games. Here challenges range from pole vaulting to hurdling to jumping to short, middle, and distance running to discus, hammer, and javelin throwing, and decathlon and heptathlon events.

Athletes from around the globe have excelled in these running, jumping, and throwing events for centuries, but one name stands out in the long, broken history of Olympic track-and-field contests. By winning four gold medals in the 1936 Berlin Games, Jesse Owens proved to both Adolf Hitler and the world that excellence is not a matter of color, but rather a matter of talent, training, and determination. In so doing, Jesse Owens became the symbol of the Olympic spirit.

In this lesson students read about a poor, sickly cotton-picking youngster who grew into a world-class athlete who set records, won medals, and promoted athletic competition as a means of combating racial tensions and promoting goodwill among all people.

Teaching Activities

Track-and-Field Fun: Students identify individual track-and-field events by description.
If at Last You Don't Succeed: Students read the inspiring story of a running star whose courage and glory could not be diminished even when cancer won the race.

Extensions

1. Stage intramural track-and-field contests among members of your class.
2. Locate and view videos of past Olympic track-and-field competitions including the 1936 Summer Games.
3. Research and report on the history of specific track-and-field events.
4. Assign individual groups of students to create charts identifying the rules and scoring guidelines for specific track-and-field events.
5. Ancient Romans included a running event in their Olympic Games in which men clad in full armor raced against one another. Pit your students against one another in a running contest wherein contestants are clad in heavy boots, snowsuits, and wrist and ankle weights.

Disproving White Supremacy

On September 12, 1913, a baby boy, who would in later years be dubbed "nonhuman" by a member of the Nazi regime, was born in Danville, Alabama. After all, James Cleveland Owens was a black child born into a society that belittled minorities with unjust laws of segregation. He was a sickly child, chronically suffering bronchial congestion and frequently battling attacks of pneumonia. He was a poor child, born to sharecroppers who could not always provide the best in food or shelter for their 11 children. Finally, he was a working child, already picking 100 pounds of cotton a day by the age of seven. Still, J. C. Owens had an extraordinary talent; and that talent would eventually catapult the poor, sickly, hardworking, black boy to victory over and over again proving to an arrogant white world that African Americans do not comprise an inferior race. The story of Jesse Owens began in Ohio in 1928. That is the year J. C. and his family migrated to Cleveland from Danville. A teacher who asked the name of her new student misinterpreted the child's Southern drawl and believed he responded with "Jesse." On that day, J. C. Owens became Jesse Owens. In days to come, Jesse Owens would become *the* Jesse Owens.

Charles Riley was the first man to recognize Jesse's unmatched ability to run. While putting together a boys' track team at Fairmount Junior High School, he timed Jesse sprinting down a city street.

Owens' speed amazed Mr. Riley, who not only gave Jesse a place on the team but also a place in his heart. Riley mentored and befriended Jesse, coaching him to run and jump, and teaching him the secrets of self-confidence, discipline, and determination. Owens was a quick learner. He led Fairmount's track team to the 1928 state championship meet where he set new world records for junior high students in both the high jump and the broad jump.

Owens continued to amaze track-and-field fans during his high-school career. He was a state champion for three consecutive years, excelling in the 100-yard dash, the 220-yard dash, and the long jump. During his senior year, Jesse set or tied three high school world records. Then challenges confronted Owens again.

Although recruited by many colleges, Jesse had to work hard to succeed at university living. Because he was black, he was not allowed to reside on the campus of Ohio State, where he attended classes. Because he was already a father and husband upon graduating from high school, he had to pump gas, wait tables, stock library shelves, and operate elevators in addition to attending school and track practice to make ends meet. Because he was not naturally skilled at academic learning, he had to study harder than many of his fellow students to succeed in college-level courses.

Still, Jesse continued to run and jump faster and farther than all of his competitors. During his junior year at Ohio State University, he won every one of the 42 events in which he competed. Then in 1935, two weeks before the Big Ten Championship Games, Jesse slipped and fell while engaged in horseplay with his teammates around a hotel room. On May 25, as the games got under way, Owens could not even bend over to tie his shoes, until it was his turn to compete. Then, miraculously, the pain disappeared, and Jesse experienced what some sports historians consider the best day any one athlete has ever experienced in a single day of track-and-field competitions. On May 25, 1935, at the Big Ten Championship Games, the "Buckeye Bullet" broke three world records and tied a fourth within 45 minutes.

Owens's most historically significant achievements, however, were yet to come. One year following the Big Ten games, Jesse Owens qualified for the U.S. Olympic track-and-field team. He prepared to compete in the 1936 Berlin Games. Adolf Hitler was determined to use the German-sponsored event to promote his Aryan supremacy theory. Months before the games even began, he and his comrades guaranteed white men and women would claim Olympic gold in competitions across the board. They ridiculed the United States for relying on "black auxiliaries" and "nonhumans" to be on the track-and-field team. Thanks to Jesse Owens, Adolf Hitler was proved wrong.

Although Hitler refused to shake his hand or hang the medal around his neck, Jesse Owens pleased a cheering crowd of thousands when he dispelled the myth of Aryan supremacy in 10.3 seconds. That is how long it took him to run the 100-meter dash. His time tied a world record and earned him a gold medal. Owens went on to win a gold in the long jump, setting an Olympic record; a gold in the 200-meter dash, setting an Olympic record; and a gold in the 400-meter relay, helping his teammates set an Olympic and world record before the 1936 Summer Games concluded.

The son of sharecroppers and grandson of slaves returned to his home country with four gold medals. Alas, the United States was little more ready for a black hero than was Hitler. Although parties were thrown in Owens's honor, he still had to ride in the backs of buses and up the cargo elevators of high-rises to get to his own parties. The president of the United States did not offer to shake Owens's hand nor even send him a card of congratulations. Because no other jobs were offered him, Jesse even had to resort to racing dogs and horses to earn money to support his family.

Somehow, Owens managed to maintain his dignity and strived to change society's perception of minorities. Organizing and managing all-black basketball and softball teams and working with underprivileged youth in the role of playground director, Jesse promoted his own theory which suggested that athletic competition could dispel racial tensions and promote goodwill among all people. Today his athletic achievements and determination to bring people of varying economic, cultural, and ethnic backgrounds together make Jesse Owens—the poor, sickly, black boy from Alabama—the symbol of the Olympic spirit.

Name ______________________________

Track-and-Field Fun

Match the track-and-field events listed below with their definitions.

DASHES	MIDDLE-DISTANCE RUNS	CROSS-COUNTRY RUN
HURDLE RACE	MARATHON RACE	RELAY RACES
STEEPLECHASE	HIGH JUMP	POLE VAULT
LONG JUMP	TRIPLE JUMP	SHOT PUT
DISCUS THROW	HAMMER THROW	JAVELIN THROW
DECATHLON	HEPTATHLON	

__________________ 1. This men's contest involves ten events completed over the course of two days. It is considered the most challenging of all Olympic competitions.

__________________ 2. These 100-, 200-, and 400-meter contests require an athlete to expend complete effort for the entire distance of the run.

__________________ 3. This obstacle race contains hurdles and water jumps among other challenges.

__________________ 4. Athletes use a long pole to help them clear a bar in this event.

__________________ 5. Athletes throw a steel-tipped metal spear in this event.

__________________ 6. Athletes sprint over 10 barriers in this short race.

__________________ 7. Competitors attempt to jump the greatest distance in this contest.

__________________ 8. Teams of four compete in these races by taking turns running a portion of the required distance before passing a baton to a teammate.

__________________ 9. The goal of this competition is to clear a crossbar that is progressively raised until only one contestant can jump the height required to achieve the feat.

__________________ 10. Races ranging from a distance of 600 meters to 3,000 meters fall into this category of runs.

__________________ 11. The competitor who throws a solid metal ball the farthest wins this competition.

__________________ 12. A jumper is allowed to hop, step, and jump in this competition.

__________________ 13. This long-distance running event occurs over rugged terrain.

__________________ 14. A hardwood or metal platter is thrown for distance in this event.

__________________ 15. This women's two-day long contest includes 100-meter hurdles, the shot put, the high jump, the long jump, a 200-meter run, and a javelin throw.

__________________ 16. This long-distance run covers more than 26 miles.

__________________ 17. The object that is thrown in this event is comprised of a ball, a length of wire, and a handle.

Name ______________________________

If at Last You Don't Succeed

Read the account of the Canadian runner Terry Fox below and then answer the questions about success and defeat that follow on your own paper.

On July 28, 1958, Terry Fox was born in Manitoba, Canada. The boy loved to participate in sports. During his elementary years, he played road hockey with his father, brothers, and friends. During his high school years, he ran races and played on his school's basketball and soccer teams. He even shared with his best friend his school's Male Athlete of the Year award during his senior year. During his college years, Fox played basketball on Simon Fraser University's junior varsity team.

Then tragedy struck. Fox woke up one morning with knee pains. When the pains became bad enough that he could not put any weight on his right leg, his father took Fox to the hospital. Fox was diagnosed with cancer of the bone. In order to save his life, Fox's doctors had to amputate Fox's leg above the knee.

Fox was determined to live a normal life after his operation. He got used to an artificial leg and returned to his normal activities. He returned to his college classes, he played golf, he managed Simon Fraser's junior varsity basketball team, and he participated in a wheelchair basketball league. Fox also took up running again.

In 1979 Fox decided that he could raise money for cancer research by getting sponsors to support him in a run that would take him from one coast of Canada to the other. For one full year, Terry trained for his transcontinental run. Although he acquired bruises and shin splints, and chafing and bleeding of his stump, Terry continued to train daily. Then on April 12, 1980, he began his "Marathon of Hope."

Fox's journey across Canada ended four months after it had begun. After 3,339 miles of running at the rate of 24 miles a day, Terry could go no farther. He had not yet reached his goal, but he was sick. Coughing and in pain, Terry completed a final mile where fans were lined up along the roadside to watch him run. Then he was rushed to the hospital.

This time Terry Fox was diagnosed with lung cancer. Although he did not run completely across the continent, Terry was rewarded for his courage and determination to raise money for cancer research. He received Canada's highest civilian honor and a number of other awards. When Fox died in June of 1981, flags were flown at half-staff on all Canadian federal buildings and military bases. A play and a movie were produced about the courageous life of Terry Fox. Through the millions of dollars donated to cancer research in his honor, Terry Fox continues to inspire people even though his life has ended.

1. Use details from the story to argue that cancer beat Terry Fox.
2. Use details from the story to argue that Terry Fox beat cancer.
3. Fox died at such a young age that he had not yet acquired a good job or made much money. He had not reached any goals in the business world. He had not even earned his college degree yet. Was Terry Fox successful? How do you define success?
4. Argue that the title of this lesson is either an appropriate or inappropriate title for the story of Terry Fox. Justify your answer with logic and details from the story.

The Other Babe

Background

American women during the first half of the twentieth century were expected to fit a stereotype. Females typically married young, raised children, and kept house. Societal pressures dictated that women wear dresses, bake cookies, and defer to the wishes of their husbands. Treated in the media and on the big screen as emotional and temperamental beings, women were not even permitted to vote in national elections until 1920.

Another field virtually closed to American women during the early part of the twentieth century was the field of athletics. High schools seldom carried girls' sports teams prior to the 1970s. Women's professional athletic leagues did not begin to appear until well into the second half of the century. Reducing the number of opportunities for women athletes even further, the Amateur Athletic Union canceled the membership of all organizations that sponsored women's teams in 1914. Athletic females who did find a forum to compete during the early and mid-twentieth century were condemned by sportscasters, newspaper editors, and even friends and acquaintances as "mannish," "unnatural," and "homosexual."

Born in 1914, one of the seven children of an athletic Norwegian family residing in southern Texas, Babe Didrikson defied stereotypes and ignored societal expectations. Didrikson could play basketball and baseball and volleyball. She excelled at swimming, diving, roller-skating, and billiards. She mastered tennis and golf. Didrikson was a world-class athlete, and she was determined to let the world know.

In this lesson students learn about a woman who symbolizes the struggle for respect endured by female athletes in America. Although she never succeeded at making women's sports as acceptable as male sports, Babe Didrikson did succeed in displaying her athletic prowess to the world, using intriguing strategies to gain the right to "play ball."

Teaching Activities

Lady Golfers Across the Ages: Students learn about historical and modern-day female golfers.

Demanding Success: Students consider situations in which they are willing to defy conventions to accomplish goals or hold on to dreams as Babe did.

Extensions

1. Research and report on other women basketball players from the Amateur Athletic Union of the 1920s and 1930s.
2. Assign reports on the statistics and lives of modern Women's National Basketball Association players.
3. Research and report on the female teams that played baseball during World War II.
4. Assign reports on other athletes who have excelled in multiple sports.
5. Organize intramural games for your students in sports in which they excel or enjoy playing.
6. Assign the creation of written, videotaped, or tape-recorded play-by-play recordings of a sporting event that takes place at your school.
7. Assign the creation of collages displaying photographs of sports figures.

Student Reading

The Other Babe

Following a phenomenal high-school basketball career in the early 1930s, Babe Didrikson did not succeed in being recruited onto a professional women's basketball team, but only because there existed no professional women's basketball team. Although an exceptional tennis player, Babe Didrikson did not succeed at playing organized tennis, but only because her amateur status was questioned and there existed no professional women's league for her to join. After qualifying to compete in five Olympic Game events, Babe Didrikson only succeeded in winning three medals, but only because women were restricted to three events for their own "safety" in the 1932 games. Although she established world records in golf that still stand today, Babe Didrikson succeeded in playing in a professional women's golf league only after she formed one herself. Although able to strike out baseball's major leaguers during training season exhibition games, Babe Didrikson did not succeed in playing on a professional baseball team, but only because there existed no professional women's baseball team. Babe Didrikson did, however, succeed in being named the Female Athlete of the Year six times. Additionally, in 1950, she was named by the Associated Press the "Greatest Athlete of the First Half of the Twentieth Century." She also succeeded in convincing some modern sports historians that Babe Didrikson was the best all-around athlete—male or female—the world has ever known.

Babe Didrikson succeeded in becoming a great and recognized athlete, not because opportunities to compete abounded for women athletes of her day, but because she was determined to play ball anyway. Born Mildred Didrikson in 1914, Babe grew up in a large, athletic family. From early childhood, Mildred ran races, rolled around on roller skates, and played volleyball and basketball in a gym her father had built in her family's backyard. Before leaving elementary school, Mildred earned the nickname "Babe" by hitting five home runs in a single baseball game. By the time she reached high school, she excelled in volleyball, tennis, baseball, basketball, and swimming.

Babe played such phenomenal basketball, in fact, that she was recruited to play on the Dallas-based Employers Casualty Insurance Company's women's team before graduating from high school. Hired as a secretary, Babe's greatest initial contribution to the insurance company was her ability to lead its Golden Cyclones in their successful quest for the national championship. Her next contribution was even more impressive. Entering the National Amateur Athletic Union track-and-field competitions as the sole member of the Golden Cyclones team in 1932 at age 18, Babe won five of the eight events she entered, breaking four world records and racking up a final score that almost doubled the score of the next closest *team,* which claimed 20 members.

Babe's accomplishments that day landed her in the media spotlight and on the 1932 U.S. Olympic track-and-field team. Although she qualified to compete in five Olympic events, she was restricted to compete in only three that year because she was a woman. At the Los Angeles Olympics, she won the javelin event gold with only one throw; won the 80-meter hurdles event, beating a world record; and tied Jean Shiley for a new world record in the high jump, claiming the silver instead of the gold only because the judges objected to her unorthodox jumping style.

Following her Olympic success, Babe barnstormed the continent with exhibition games in basketball, baseball, and tennis. She astonished vaudeville crowds and sports fans with her abilities in bowling, rifle shooting, diving, swimming, roller-skating, and volleyball. Although there were few opportunities during the mid-twentieth century for women to play on professional athletic teams, and although women who did compete in sports were considered "mannish" and "freakish," Babe Didrikson was determined to succeed in the world of sports. When opportunities did not present themselves for her to compete, Didrikson created them. She challenged Babe Ruth to exhibition games of golf. She struck out Lou Gehrig in a spring training exhibition baseball game. She formed a traveling basketball team that challenged men on the back roads of America to popular and competitive games of ball played in their own community gyms. Finally, she settled into a single-sport niche.

Upon the suggestion of a media sportswriter who admired Babe's astonishing all-around athletic prowess, Didrikson learned to play golf in 1933. Hitting thousands of balls for eight hours daily until her hands blistered and bled, Babe taught herself to drive a golf ball 250 yards on a consistent basis. Within a year after learning to play the game, she was winning amateur tournaments. In all, Babe Didrikson won over 80 golf tournaments. In 1945 she won every single golf game she played. From 1946 to 1947 she won 17 consecutive amateur tournaments, a feat no golfer of either sex has ever matched. In 1948 Didrikson founded the Ladies Professional Golf Association and went on to win 31 LPGA events. Babe won several of her final tournaments in spite of suffering the pain of colon cancer.

Then on September 27, 1956, Babe Didrikson succumbed to cancer. She was only 42 years old at the time of her death, but one of the greatest athletes this world has ever known packed a full life into her short years on earth.

Name ____________________

Lady Golfers Across the Ages

Based on the information that follows about the history of women's golf and the accomplishments of female golfers from the past and present, create a poster promoting the Ladies Professional Golf Association on a large piece of poster board. Include drawings, a summarized history of women's golf, highlights of the careers of golfers presented below (plus any other women golfers you may wish to include), and a fictional tournament schedule listing times and places of future LPGA play.

WOMEN'S GOLF IN HISTORY
Women's competitive golf was organized as early as 1890, but it would be decades before it became socially acceptable. Women were not allowed on many golf courses in the early days of women's golf, and when they were permitted to play, they were expected to wear high collars, long sleeves, and dresses.

MARY, QUEEN OF SCOTS
The sixteenth-century Queen of Scots was one of the first recognized women in history to enjoy playing golf. Queen Mary has also been credited with introducing the caddy to the game, since she required her "cadets" to carry her clubs for her on the golf course.

Unfortunately, golf contributed to Queen Mary's demise. When she played a few holes of the game immediately following her second husband's death, her "unmournful" behavior added to already existing suspicions that she had killed her spouse. Thanks to an untimely nine holes, Queen Mary was convicted and beheaded in 1587.

ISSETTE PEARSON
In 1893 Issette Pearson of London, England, formed the Ladies Golf Union dedicated to developing a handicapping system, establishing uniform rules, and organizing an annual women's golfing championship tournament.

JOYCE WETHERED
Joyce Wethered was one of the first well-known female golfers in the United States. Although completing only one golf lesson as a child, she won four British Open Amateur competitions and five English championships. She was considered by many during her day, the greatest golfer of either sex.

MODERN-DAY WOMEN GOLFERS
KARRIE WEBB
Karrie Webb has been playing golf professionally since 1996 when she was awarded the Rookie Female Golfer of the Year award. She qualified for the LPGA tour on her first attempt even while playing with a broken wrist. She achieved 16 career victories from 1996-1999.

ANNIKA SÖRENSTAM
Annika Sörenstam began playing golf in her native Sweden at the age of 12. In 1992 she earned the title of World Amateur Champion. In 1993 she won the WPG European tour and was named European Rookie of the Year before joining the LPGA. Annika won the U.S. Open in both 1995 and 1996.

Name ______________________________

Demanding Success

Babe Didrikson succeeded in making sports her life only because she was determined to do so. Female athletes found few opportunities to compete during her day. What do you value so strongly that you are willing to defy modern conventions to make it a part of your life? Discuss the questions below with two or three other students and then record your individual answers below.

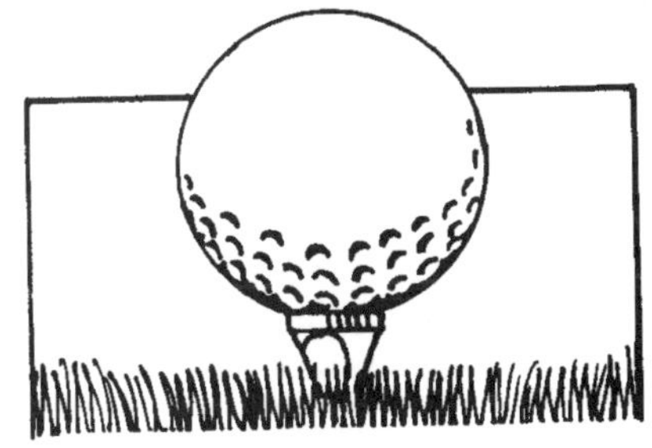

1. What activities do you engage in that are not considered "cool" by some of the students at your school? How do you deal with rude comments from others about your participation in that activity?

 ____

 ____

 ____

2. What activities are you good at that are not always considered activities suited for your sex? For example are you an exceptional male cook or seamstress? Are you a female who excels in football? Do your friends know you are good at the skills you listed? Are you willing to participate in public in those activities you listed? Why or why not?

 ____

 ____

 ____

3. What beliefs or values do you hold that are unpopular with some of the people at your school (i.e., religious or spiritual beliefs, beliefs in UFOs or aliens, valuing abstinence, or academic honesty)? Do your friends know what you value and believe? Do lesser-known acquaintances know what you value and believe? Why or why not? How do you deal with negative comments from other people about your belief system?

 ____

 ____

 ____

4. Do you have any dreams about your future that you think are too unrealistic or outrageous to tell a friend about? If you were determined to make those dreams come true, how would you go about doing so? Are you willing to try to reach those dreams? Why or why not?

 ____

 ____

 ____

Diving for Gold

Background

"Fancy" or competitive diving is over 300 years old. Seventeenth-century German and Swedish gymnasts used to move their equipment to beachfronts during summer months so they could include water acrobatics in their performances. Out of such acrobatic water shows developed the sport of competitive diving.

Fancy diving gained Olympic status around the turn of the century when men's platform competitions were first included in the 1904 games held in St. Louis. Men's springboard diving was added in 1908. Women began diving in the Olympics in 1912. Although the Swedes and Germans dominated the Olympic sport of diving for the first several years, the Americans have been doing so consistently since 1920. In fact, the United States experiences more medal-winning success in diving than in any other Olympic competition.

Modern American diving competitions are regulated by United States Diving, Incorporated. Whereas early twentieth-century divers had 14 official basic platform dives and 20 official basic springboard dives to choose from in competitions, United States Diving, Incorporated currently lists a total of 204 dive variations. While forward double somersaults were at the top of the difficulty chart in 1904, Greg Louganis nailed a reverse 3½ somersault to claim his fourth gold medal in 1988.

In this lesson students read about the challenges in the life of the first man in history to win the gold medal in both the springboard and platform competitions during two consecutive Olympics. In so doing, they tackle the difficult issues of AIDS and drug abuse that have plagued the phenomenal athlete, Greg Louganis.

Teaching Activities

Name That Dive: Students learn about dives, body positioning, and scoring in competitive diving.
Splashing Good Athletes: Students read about Olympic divers and diving coaches from history.

Extensions

1. Require students to research and report on other Olympic competition sports.
2. Assign the creation of posters illustrating the various body positions and dives listed in the Name That Dive activity.
3. Show your class a video of competitive diving and allow students to act as judges as they watch the athletes compete.
4. Assign the writing of an essay comparing and contrasting diving with its predecessor, gymnastics.
5. Research and report on the latest medical news about AIDS.
6. Assign reports on other famous athletes who have overcome drug abuse or suffered through AIDS or another life-threatening illness.

Student Reading

Diving for Gold

On January 26, 1960, a 15-year-old San Diego resident gave birth to a baby boy. After spending nine months with the child, the young girl—along with the boy's 15-year-old father—gave up Greg Louganis for adoption. The child's adoptive parents loved and cared for him kindly, but Greg's early years were challenging just the same. Children in Greg's elementary school made fun of him because his skin was dark. They made fun of him because he suffered dyslexia and had trouble reading. They made fun of him because he attended dance and gymnastics classes after school hours.

Greg's father marveled at his son's dance and gymnastic abilities. When Greg starting doing tumbles off the end of the diving board at the family pool, he enrolled Greg in one more athletic activity—diving lessons. Schoolmates would soon-after stop laughing at Greg Louganis.

In 1971 the 11-year-old child, who had completed just two years of diving lessons, found himself competing in the Junior Olympics in Colorado Springs. One of his dives earned him national recognition when it scored a perfect 10. Louganis could easily have been on his way to athletic greatness, but not yet. Suffering a low self-image, perhaps in connection with the ridicule he had endured in elementary school, Greg began doing speed and selling marijuana at the age of 12.

Gratefully, the thrill of competitive diving gradually replaced the artificially induced high of doing and selling drugs. By 1975 Greg was clean and happy. Recognizing and respecting his own talent by then, the 15-year-old began training with Dr. Sammy Lee, an Olympic gold medalist and accomplished coach. The next year Greg Louganis represented the United States in the Montreal Olympics. He placed sixth in springboard diving and brought home a silver medal from the platform competition.

The nation was proud of the 16-year-old boy, but Greg was not proud of himself. He felt he had failed in his first Olympic showing, and this time he turned to alcohol and cigarettes. For about the next five years, Greg continued to drink, smoke, and win numerous world titles and championships in diving. Sports analysts suggested he would have had a good shot at the gold medal in the 1980 Olympics, too, had the United States not boycotted the games in response to the Soviet Union's invasion of Afghanistan. Still, Greg later contended that the missed Olympic opportunity gave him time to mature as a diver and as a person. Around 1982 Greg broke his smoking and drinking habits and concentrated exclusively on his talents. He earned his bachelor of arts degree in theater from the University of California in Irvine and became the first diver to ever receive a perfect "10" from all seven judges in a major competition.

By the time the next Olympic opportunity rolled around, Greg Louganis had learned to appreciate both his talents and himself. This time he dived his way to gold in both the platform and springboard competitions. Additionally, he became the first diver to receive more than 700 points in a single Olympic Game.

His accomplishments earned Louganis the 1984 Sullivan Award, which is presented to America's best amateur athlete of the year. It also ensured his place on the 1988 United States Olympic diving team. If Louganis could win the gold medal in both the springboard and platform competition again in 1988, he would be the first male diver in Olympic history to win consecutive golds in both competitions.

The prospects for doing so, however, did not look good. Although Louganis had not yet acknowledged it publicly, he had been diagnosed with the HIV virus before the 1988 games in Seoul. The emotional strain of that private knowledge must have been difficult even before the accident, but then it happened. While executing a reverse 2½ somersault pike in the springboard preliminaries, Louganis hit the back of his head on the board. Fear and embarrassment enveloped Louganis. He later expressed that the two thoughts running through his mind immediately following the mishap were, "What if I bled in the pool?" and "How do I get out of the water with no one noticing my embarrassment?"

All questions were answered. Louganis had not bled in the pool. No one noticed Louganis's embarrassment as they feared for his safety. And Louganis was able to continue the competition—and qualify for the finals—following a 35-minute break in which he received temporary stitches in the back of the head. Engrossed in close competition with the 14-year-old Xiong Ni of China until the very last of the platform dives, the stitched-up Greg Louganis would have to nail a near perfect "death dive," a reverse 3½ somersault, if he were to achieve his goal of back-to-back Olympic golds in both diving events. Gracefully, he executed the "death dive" and moved ahead of Xiong Ni by 1.14 points. Greg Louganis became the first male diver in Olympic history to walk away with his fourth gold medal—all earned in consecutive springboard and platform competitions.

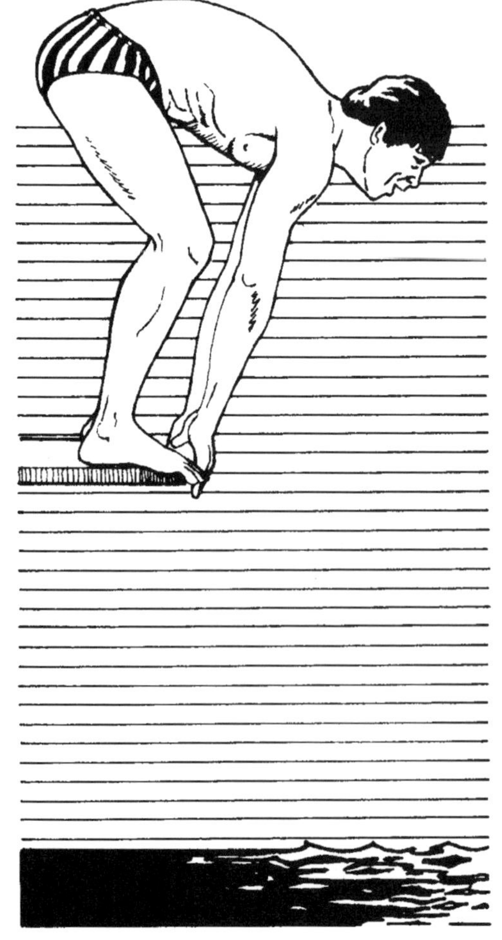

The next year Greg Louganis announced his retirement from diving competition. Today he acts in stage shows and speaks to young people about drug and alcohol rehabilitation. Although AIDS may claim the life of Louganis before he reaches his golden years, nothing can take away the impact of the man who, through courage and self-acceptance, overcame childhood ridicule, teenage drug abuse, and an ostracizing illness to become one of the most respected and accomplished athletes in Olympic history.

Name ______________________________

Name That Dive

Use your understanding of vocabulary and an encyclopedia to help you define the diving terms below.

I. DIVING VARIETIES

______ 1. Forward, backward, reverse, or inward dives that include a twist fall into this diving category.

______ 2. When executing this dive, the diver bends forward to clasp ankles at the highest point of the dive before straightening back out before hitting the water.

______ 3. Everything from a simple front dive to the forward 3½ somersault fit into this category of dives.

______ 4. In this dive, the diver holds his/her arms straight out to the sides until nearing the water at which time they are brought together.

______ 5. Also called a cutaway, this dive finds the diver standing backwards on the board, jumping off, and spinning back toward the board before entering the water head first.

______ 6. When divers begin a dive standing on the board with their backs toward the water, their dives fall into this category.

______ 7. Also called a gainer, this dive begins with the diver facing the water until takeoff when he or she rotates back toward the board in a half somersault.

A. Swan dive
B. Forward
C. Backward
D. Jackknife
E. Reverse
F. Inward
G. Twisting

II. BODY POSITION VARIATIONS

______ 1. In this position, a diver's legs are straight while the body is bent at the waist.

______ 2. This term refers to a combination of positions used in twisting dives.

______ 3. The diver does not bend at the knees or waist in this position.

______ 4. The legs are drawn to the chest and the heels are close to the bottom in this diving position.

A. Straight
B. Pike
C. Tuck
D. Free

III. JUDGING CONSIDERATIONS

______ 1. Judges look for a tiny splash and a vertical angle when judging this last stage of a dive.

______ 2. A judge hopes to see a smooth, confident walk when judging this first stage of a dive.

______ 3. Judges consider mechanics, technique, and style when deciding on a grade for this judging category.

______ 4. Judges consider angle, control, and balance during this stage of a dive.

______ 5. This term refers to the amount of lift a diver achieves.

A. Approach
B. Takeoff
C. Elevation
D. Execution
E. Entry

Name ________________________________

Splashing Good Athletes

Use the Internet or a reference book on Olympic medal winners to help you determine which of the following statements about Olympic divers are true. Indicate your responses with a "T" for true or an "F" for false.

________ 1. Dr. Sammy Lee, the renowned coach who worked with Pat McCormick, Greg Louganis, and others never participated in Olympic diving competitions himself.

________ 2. Klaus Diblasi is the Italian diver who won the gold medal in platform diving in 1976, the year Louganis took the silver.

________ 3. Aileen Riggin, a gold medal diver, was once coached by her husband, Glen McCormick.

________ 4. Vickie Draves became the first person to win both the platform and springboard gold medals in 1948.

________ 5. Pat McCormick was the first diver to win back-to-back gold medals in both platform and springboard competitions in two consecutive Olympics. Greg Louganis was the second to accomplish the feat. No woman besides Pat has ever achieved the same.

________ 6. Aileen Riggin became the first United States springboard gold medalist in 1920.

________ 7. Giorgio Cagnotto won four medals (two silver and two bronze) over the course of three decades from 1964 through 1980.

________ 8. In addition to his four Olympic gold medals, Greg Louganis has held five world championship titles and 47 national titles.

________ 9. Frank Dempsey won four gold medals in diving events from 1942–1946.

________10. Dmitry Sautin became the first Chinese male to ever win the men's platform gold medal in 1996.

________11. If China's Xiao Hailiang had won the platform diving gold in the 1996 Olympics, China would have become the second country to sweep all of the diving event gold medals in one Olympic Game. Because Xiao took the bronze medal, the United States is the only country to have accomplished this feat—in 1952.

________12. David Pichler of the United States won the springboard gold medal at the 1996 Olympic Games.

Answer Key

TILTING AT WINDMILLS

Modern Adventures page 8

Accept all reasonable responses.

Defining Descriptions page 9

1. campground
2. city
3. library
4. classroom
5. movie theater

RAGS TO RICHES: A FAIRY-TALE LIFE

Mr. Andersen or Brothers Grimm page 12

1. B, Andersen
2. D, Andersen
3. I, Andersen
4. A, Grimm Brothers
5. E, Andersen
6. G, Andersen
7. J, Grimm Brothers
8. F, Grimm Brothers
9. C, Grimm Brothers
10. H, Andersen

From Fact to Fairy Tale page 13

1. Hans Christian Andersen spent his childhood in poverty but went on to become very successful not because he was from a wealthy family with a good name, or even because he was exceptionally intelligent, but rather because he was a hard worker who believed in his own dreams.
2. Hans Christian Andersen was never married, but stories of his life suggest he was in love at least three times. Perhaps he was painfully rejected, causing him to have a negative impression of Cupid.
3. Hans Christian Andersen was a dreamer whose belief in fairy-tale endings angered and frustrated some of the people in his life. Many people along the way advised Andersen to learn a trade, but eventually, he made them all see his dreams as clearly as he did. Incidentally, like the boy in the story, Andersen was a very good artist. Some of his paper clipping art hangs in the house where he grew up, which now serves as the Hans Christian Andersen museum.
4. "The Gardener and the Fine Family" reflects the fact that Hans Christian Andersen became famous in several other European countries before his home country of Denmark would accept him as a respected author.

Light Tale, Deep Truths page 14

Grade according to predetermined criteria for the writing of a fairy tale.

UNWELCOME SLEUTH SUCCESS

Detecting Truths page 18

2. True: Since he wrote the first detective story, Edgar Allan Poe is considered the father of the genre.
3. True: Authors before Doyle used many of the writing techniques Doyle employed.
4. False: The setting and characters in the Sherlock Holmes stories reflect a profound understanding of Victorian England and Doyle's immediate world.
5. False: Short story writing was only one facet of Doyle's varied life as indicated by the diversity of activities mentioned in the paragraph presented.

Conan Contemporaries page 19

1. Rudyard Kipling
2. James Joyce
3. D. H. Lawrence
4. Elizabeth Barrett Browning
5. Virginia Woolf
6. Lord Alfred Tennyson
7. Charles Dickens
8. George Eliot
9. H. G. Wells
10. Lewis Carroll

THE WORLD IS MY HOME

Panoramic Views page 23

Accept all reasonable responses.

Name That Epic page 24

1. O
2. F
3. A
4. C
5. G
6. D
7. H
8. E
9. J
10. L
11. I
12. K
13. M
14. P
15. N
16. B

ACCLAIM AND CONTROVERSY

On the Shoulders of Giants page 29

1. Emily Dickinson
2. Leo Tolstoy
3. Doris Lessing
4. The Brontë Sisters
5. E. E. Cummings
6. William Faulkner
7. Fyodor Dostoevsky
8. Albert Camus
9. Gwendolyn Brooks
10. Bessie Head

Walker Contemporaries page 30

1. Ralph Ellison
2. Richard Wright
3. Zora Neale Hurston
4. Langston Hughes
5. James Baldwin
6. Maya Angelou
7. Toni Morrison

A "PAINE"FUL LIFE

Paine Talk page 34

1. *The American Crisis*
2. *The American Crisis*
3. *Common Sense*
4. *The Rights of Man*
5. *The Age of Reason*
6. *The Rights of Man*
7. *Common Sense*
8. *The American Crisis*
9. *Common Sense*
10. *The American Crisis*
11. *The Age of Reason*
12. *The Age of Reason*

Fightin' Words page 35

Accept all responses.

HONEST ABE

Lincoln Family Photos pages 38 and 39

Establish guidelines for the construction of the photo albums before students begin work on this assignment.

Storyteller page 40

Story One: Fact (probably): Although it is uncertain whether this particular story about Mr. Lincoln's honesty and superior customer service is true, several similar stories suggest he did do many kind acts while employed under Mr. Offutt.

Story Two: Fact: This story has been verified by others in the town of New Salem.

Story Three: Fact or Fiction: Historians argue about the validity of this story. Although the letter does exist, Mr. Lincoln may have been simply jesting his friend as he was wont to do.

Story Four: Fact: The stories of Lincoln splitting railroad ties are true.

Story Five: Fact: A warrant was written for the arrest of Lincoln, but it was determined that he was not breaking any laws with his business that ushered customers from shore to another boat at mid-river.

Story Six: Fact: This story has been retold in several biographies about Lincoln.

Story Seven: Fact: Lincoln loved to tell stories.

Story Eight: Fact: Lincoln studied law on his own, and several accounts suggest he did so outdoors during his free time.

Story Nine: Fact: Like all lawyers of his day, Lincoln was called upon to improvise from time to time since the travels involved in circuit courts did not allow attorneys to become familiar with all elements of all cases before trial time.

SISTER STRIKE

Jones' Work in West Virginia page 43

Accept all reasonable responses.

Creating Coal page 44

1. T
2. T
3. F—Most coal mined today was formed hundreds of millions of years ago.

4. F—Although the countries that comprise the former USSR do produce more coal than the United States, the United States has a higher percentage of recoverable coal resources.
5. T
6. T
7. T
8. F—Although underground mines exist that do require miners to go below the earth's surface to collect coal, most coal is mined from surface mines today.
9. T
10. F—The process described is called continuous mining. In conventional mining, miners cut the coal with undercutters, drill holes into it with hydraulic drills, load the holes with explosives, and blast the coal into pieces before loading it into shuttle cars.
11. T
12. T
13. T
14. F—Although labor conditions for miners improved following Mother Jones' fight for their rights in the early 1900s, the Federal Mines Health and Safety Act was not passed until 1969.
15. F—Although smokestack scrubbers do protect the atmosphere, most coal-burning plants do not use them because of their great expense.
16. F—Fluidized bed combustion is used by some plants not because it is inexpensive but because it burns coal without producing airborne pollutants.
17. T
18. T
19. T
20. F—Coal tar pitch is used in the production of steel, coal, coke, and electrodes.

THE NONVIOLENT GRAY PANTHERS

Gray Panther Chronology **page 47**

Accept all illustrated, sequential time lines.

Growing Old **page 48**

1. False—A mouse is considered very old at the age of three, whereas a dog can live until it is 15 or older.
2. False—Although the metabolic rate and the mean resting heart rate decrease in old age, oxygen intake remains the same.
3. True
4. False—Although cells throughout the body do die, only some of them are irreplaceable. The cells that die in the nervous system and heart, for example, are not replaced; but the cells that die in the skin and digestive tract are replaced.
5. True
6. False—According to the AARP survey, grandparents most want to pass on to their grandchildren a sense of moral integrity—ambition comes in second.
7. True
8. True
9. True
10. False—Nine percent of elderly people describe their health as poor.
11. False—Only about 5% of the nation's elderly live in institutions.
12. True
13. True
14. False—Social Security benefits are not withheld from individuals who are collecting pensions from former employers.

Consultation of Old and Young **page 49**

There are no right or wrong answers to this exercise. It is designed to allow children and adults to cooperate on solving a single problem.

SHINING LIGHT INTO THE NIGHT

Initiating Dialogue **page 53**

1. Wiesel fears that discussing the Holocaust dishonors its victims because words tend to trivialize an event too horrific for verbal description. Wiesel feels it is necessary to discuss the Holocaust, nevertheless, because doing so may prevent unnecessary deaths in the future.
2. Accept all reasonable responses.
3. Concerned citizens can promote peace around the world by maintaining an awareness of happenings around the globe and encouraging and supporting groups that strive toward making or keeping peace. Students can promote peace in the classroom by practicing acceptance and compassion.
4. Perhaps it is difficult for those who did not experience the Holocaust to discuss it due to feelings of guilt, shame, or embarrassment that another human being had to live in such ways.
5. Accept all reasonable responses.

And the World Remained Silent **page 54**

1-2. Accept all reasonable responses.

3. The following events foreshadowed the establishment of concentration camps: discriminatory laws and taxes against Jews in Germany beginning in January 1933, the "Night of Broken Glass" event, the invasion of Poland and the establishment of fenced-off ghettos, the deporting of Jews from occupied countries to ghettos in Poland, the yellow badge requirement of Jews in Germany, and the deportation of German Jews to Poland.

MISS ELIZABETH BLACKWELL M.D.

Doctor Blackwell's Day **page 58**

Accept all well-researched responses.

Women at Work **page 59**

Set criteria for persuasive essays before students begin work.

MR. CHOCOLATE KISS

The Mennonite Way **page 63**

1. Hershey's hard work, belief in the "inner voice" that destined him to be a candymaker, and his dedication to the well-being of the members of his community all reflected his Mennonite upbringing.
2. Hershey's use of modern technology and concern about such "frivolous" things as parks and candies did not reflect Mennonite philosophy.

The Town That Milt Built **page 64**

Accept all responses that illustrate the events presented in chronological order. The events in the development of the school should include its founding and first four students, its endowment, its continued use as a facility to educate children over the years, and its current population of 1,100 children. The events in the development of Hersheypark should include all additions made to the park as presented by year.

BANKING THAT BUILDS

Earthquake! **page 67**

Evaluate according to your class's nonfiction writing stipulations.

Banking on Your Arithmetic Skills **page 68**

Scenario One

1. $424.50
2. $515.00
3. Second month
4. You would have $1.00 more at the end of the two-month period.

Scenario Two

1. Choose the high interest account because you do not intend to take out money for three years.

Scenario Three

Ending Balance: $2,202.83

THE COLONEL OF CHICKEN

Business Alternatives **page 71**

	Advantages		Disadvantages
1.	Sole Proprietorship	1.	Corporation
2.	Corporation	2.	Sole Proprietorship
3.	Sole Proprietorship	3.	Partnership
4.	Corporation	4.	Corporation
5.	Partnership	5.	Corporation
		6.	Sole Proprietorship

Keeping Secrets **page 72**

Answers will reflect student opinion, but some ideas are listed here:

1. Keeping the Colonel's recipe a secret is good for business because it ensures that nonfranchised restaurants will not use it and also serves as a good advertising point.
2. Perhaps good secrets are so much fun because they allow us to anticipate fun before it even begins.
3. Government secrets can protect the safety of a nation, but they can also serve to deceive or mislead a nation's citizens or cover up governmental fraud.
4. Secrets can hurt others when you share a negative comment about one person with another person. Secrets can also hurt others when they take the form of untrue rumors. It is best to confront people with your concerns rather than keep secrets behind their backs.
5. Secrets that create harm should never be kept. This includes the type listed in answer #4 as well as secrets of abuse or addiction that could be professionally handled if they were out in the open.
6. Student opinion will dictate this answer; however, you many wish to remind students that when a friend tells them a secret that they feel an adult should know about, they can be honest with their friend by telling him or her that they will not be able to keep the secret completely confidential, but will be sharing it with one trusted adult.

THE SUPERCOMPUTER OF A SUPERBRAIN

Mrs. Emeagwali **page 76**

1. Roald Dahl achieved success in writing adult and children's fiction. Patricia O'Neal is a successful actress.
2. Georgia O'Keeffe was a famous painter. Alfred Stieglitz was a successful photographer and art gallery director.
3. Pierre and Marie Curie were famous scientists who worked together.
4. Elizabeth Barrett Browning and Robert Browning were both authors. Elizabeth achieved much greater success than her husband during their lifetimes. Robert has become more critically acclaimed since their deaths.
5. Jane Fonda is a successful movie actress and political activist. Ted Turner is a multimillion-dollar media mogul.

The Mind of a Scientist **page 77**

Accept all reasonable responses reported in complete sentences.

Role-Playing Greatness **page 78**

Accept all accurate portrayals.

THE GREATEST SHOWMAN ON EARTH

Barnum's Menagerie **pages 82 and 83**

Student essays will vary.

Under the Big Top **page 84**

1. True
2. False—The first circus acts were displays of horsemanship.
3. False—The first circus was organized by a former English cavalry man who performed horsemanship in England in 1768, and then later throughout Europe.
4. True
5. False—The first circus man to perform in the United States was John Bill Ricketts, a horseback rider who displayed his tricks in 1792 in Philadelphia.
6. True—Although a free-will offering was collected, the first circuses were free.
7. True
8. True—The first to do so was William Cameron Coup who operated a two-ring circus in 1869. P. T. Barnum partnered with Coup when he first entered the circus world.
9. True
10. True
11. False—Canada is home to the most popular circus of modern times, the Cirque du Soleil.
12. True—By the time Barnum joined Bailey, Phineas was an old man who had slowed down a bit. Bailey was the mastermind behind their enterprise. It has been said that army leaders required their recruits to watch Bailey pack up a circus in an attempt to teach the men to pack and travel with efficiency.

PICTURE PERFECT

Visualizing Beauty **page 88**

Accept all student artwork.

"Mr. O'Keeffe" **page 89**

1. Auguste Rodin
2. John Marin
3. Edward Steichen
4. Pablo Picasso, Henri Rousseau
5. Ansel Adams
6. Paul Cézanne, Henri Matisse
7. Arthur Dove
8. Marsden Hartley

AMERICAN AMBASSADOR OF JAZZ

All That Jazz **page 93**

1. This original jazz style showcased a cornet melody echoed by a clarinet countermelody, supported by the low sounds of trombone and tuba, and rhythmically supported by a string bass and drums.
2. This term describes music played in the New Orleans style by white musicians.
3. This music derived from the New Orleans Jazz placed more emphasis on soloists and added saxophones to the sound.
4. This 1970's style featured scores that included long stretches of music in a single key, chord, or mode.
5. This music of the 1960s drew ideas from modern dance, pop, and soul music, as well as musical themes from different cultures, and fused them with jazz in an attempt to win an audience for jazz in a day when it was losing popularity.
6. This musical style, which was born in New York, married blues vocals with jazz instrumentals.
7. This jazz style, popularized in the 1920s, emphasized call-and-response patterns between brass and reed instruments overlaid with improvised brass solos.
8. This rejection of the big band style led by Charlie Parker and Dizzy Gillespie returned to small group performances that emphasized solo work. Adopted by many jazz artists in the 1940s and 1950s, the erratic rhythms of the new jazz form made it unsuitable for dancing and unpopular with the mainstream.
9. This 1950's musical style combined jazz techniques with classical music forms.
10. Count Basie led this renaissance in jazz focusing on the big band sound at the same time that Miles Davis fused the rock sound of stars like James Brown with jazz as he led the Fusion Jazz movement.
11. This 1950's jazz style was much like swing music but without the strong emphasis on call-and-response patterns and repeated motifs.

Jazz Greats **page 94**

Determine criteria for successful reports before students begin the assignment.

"HELLO, I'M JOHNNY CASH"

Country Music Legends **page 98**

Accept all quiz questions and answers that reflect an understanding of the facts presented.

Sharing the Wealth page 99

2. Perhaps Johnny Cash supports youth organizations because he appreciates the support he received from adults such as his mother and short-term vocal teacher in his own youth.
3. Johnny Cash probably supports prison programs because he has been jailed seven times and understands the feeling of despair that accompanies imprisonment.
4. Being happily married for years himself, Mr. Cash may support women's shelters both in gratitude to his own wife who helped him out of his addictions and in support of other women who continue to deal with addictive and abusive men.
5. Johnny Cash probably supports Christian groups because he credits his faith with helping him overcome his addictions.
6. Johnny Cash is probably concerned about the plight of many impoverished and ill-treated groups of people because he understands poverty from his own youth.
7. Perhaps Mr. Cash supports mental health institutions because he understands the connection between mental health and addictions.

SLY GUY

Access Denied page 103

Part A:

1. K	6. A	11. J
2. G	7. I	12. B
3. M	8. L	13. F
4. N	9. D	14. C
5. H	10. E	15. O

Part B: Accept all reasonable responses.

Hollywood History page 104

1. T
2. T
3. F—Although Edison is credited by some as the inventor of the kinescope, most historians believe it was really created by his assistant, William K. L. Dickson.
4. F—The first films depicted motion without a storyline (people walking, waves crashing etc.).
5. T
6. F—The first major American film was titled *The Great Train Robbery.*
7. T
8. F *The Birth of a Nation* was a controversial film due to its sympathetic treatment of the Ku Klux Klan.
9. T
10. T
11. F—The first Hollywood sign, constructed in 1923 to read Hollywoodland, advertised a housing development. It was expected to remain in use for no longer than a year and a half.
12. T
13. T
14. T
15. T
16. T
17. F—The first international renowned movie actor was Charlie Chaplin.
18. T
19. F—Although experiments were conducted in color film as early as 1906, the first motion picture to be produced in true Technicolor was the 1935 film *Becky Sharp.*
20. T

SULTAN OF SWAT

Batting to Beat the Babe page 108

1. Mark McGwire
2. Joe DiMaggio
3. Rogers Hornsby
4. Roger Maris
5. Sammy Sosa
6. Lou Gehrig
7. Ernie Banks
8. Ken Griffey, Jr.
9. Hack Wilson
10. Hank Greenberg
11. Jimmie Foxx
12. Willie Mays
13. Hank Aaron

DISPROVING WHITE SUPREMACY

Track-and-Field Fun page 113

1. Decathlon
2. Dashes
3. Steeplechase
4. Pole Vault
5. Javelin Throw
6. Hurdle Race
7. Long Jump
8. Relay Races
9. High Jump
10. Middle-Distance Runs
11. Shot Put
12. Triple Jump
13. Cross-Country Run
14. Discus Throw
15. Heptathlon
16. Marathon
17. Hammer Throw

If at Last You Don't Succeed page 114

1. Cancer beat Terry by giving him pain. claiming his right leg below the knee, ending his run across Canada, and taking his life.
2. Terry beat cancer by making his short life count. He raised millions of dollars for cancer research, inspired physically challenged people to live full lives, and brought hope to a sometimes cynical world.
3. and 4. These questions are based on student opinion. Accept all reasonable and logically justified responses.

THE OTHER BABE

Lady Golfers Across the Ages page 118

Accept all posters that demonstrate effort and understanding of the assignment.

Demanding Success page 119

Accept all answers that demonstrate critical thinking.

DIVING FOR GOLD

Name that Dive page 123

I. 1. G
 2. D
 3. B
 4. A
 5. F
 6. C
 7. E

II. 1. B
 2. D
 3. A
 4. C

III. 1. E
 2. A
 3. D
 4. B
 5. C

Splashing Good Athletes page 124

1. False—Sammy Lee won platform gold medals at the 1952 and 1956 Olympics.
2. True
3. False—Aileen was never coached by her husband, although Pat McCormick was in 1956.
4. True
5. True
6. True
7. True
8. True
9. False—Frank Dempsey won four United States national championships from 1942-1943.
10. False—Dmitry Sautin became the first Russian to win a platform gold.
11. True
12. False—For the first year since 1912, no United States divers took medals at the 1996 Olympic Games. David Pichler came in sixth in the platform competition. Xiong Ni of China won the gold.